To:

BG Grigsby,

with best wishes and thanks
for all of your support and help.

DJNeal . Sept 2012.

From Battlefield to Boardroom

The economic crash of 2008 has left a turbulent, complex and highly volatile environment, marked by uncertainty and ambiguity. As the global shareholder value economic model teeters on the edge of destruction, our organizations and institutions need different kinds of leaders. We need outstanding men and women who hold a wider perspective but one balanced by an inclusive narrative that resonates with communities.

For many years the military has identified, selected and trained such leaders, men and women who are capable of leading their fellow citizens through the most demanding of situations. This book draws deeply on the military experience and examines the qualities and capabilities underpinning values-based leadership. Wealth creation supportive of shared social values will be the leadership challenge for the future.

From Battlefield to Boardroom

Making the difference through values-based leadership

Ivan Yardley
Visiting Research Fellow, Defence Academy of the United Kingdom, Cranfield University, UK

Andrew Kakabadse
Professor of International Management Development, Cranfield School of Management, Cranfield University, UK

and

Derrick Neal
Professor of Defence Strategic Change, Defence Academy of the United Kingdom, Cranfield University, UK

First published 2012 by
PALGRAVE MACMILLAN

Palgrave Macmillan in the UK is an imprint of Macmillan Publishers Limited,
registered in England, company number 785998, of Houndmills, Basingstoke,
Hampshire RG21 6XS.

Palgrave Macmillan in the US is a division of St Martin's Press LLC,
175 Fifth Avenue, New York, NY 10010.

Palgrave Macmillan is the global academic imprint of the above companies
and has companies and representatives throughout the world.

Palgrave® and Macmillan® are registered trademarks in the United States,
the United Kingdom, Europe and other countries.

ISBN 978–0–230–29845–3

This book is printed on paper suitable for recycling and made from fully
managed and sustained forest sources. Logging, pulping and manufacturing
processes are expected to conform to the environmental regulations of the
country of origin.

A catalogue record for this book is available from the British Library.

A catalog record for this book is available from the Library of Congress.

10 9 8 7 6 5 4 3 2 1
21 20 19 18 17 16 15 14 13 12

Printed and bound in Great Britain by
CPI Antony Rowe, Chippenham and Eastbourne

Contents

LIST OF FIGURES AND BOXES

Figures

Boxes

LIST OF ABBREVIATIONS

AOSB	Army Officers Selection Board
CEO	Chief Executive Officer
CoA	Course of Action
DLOD	Defense Lines of Development
EU	European Union
FLC	Front Line Command
GE	General Electric
GFC	Global Financial Crisis
IED	Improvized Explosive Device
IPT	Integrated Project Team
MBA	Masters in Business Administration
MoD	Ministry of Defence (UK)
NATO	North Atlantic Treaty Organization
NCO	Non-Commissioned Officer
NGO	Non-Governmental Organization
NHS	National Health Service (UK)
OODA	Observation, Orientation, Decision, and Action
OUTC	Officer University Training Corp
PFI	Private Finance Initiatives
PPP	Public–Private Partnerships
PSO	Peace Support Operations
R&D	Research and Development
RBV	Resource-Based View
SOP	Standard Operational Procedure

TEPIDOIL Training, Equipment, Personnel, Infrastructure, Doctrine/Concepts, Organization, Information and Logistics
UN   United Nations
UOR   Urgent Operational Requirement
WWW   World Wide Web

FOREWORD BY LIEUTENANT GENERAL DAVID G. PERKINS

In the quest for more effective processes, efficient systems, and enhanced management practises, the military frequently finds itself incorporating tools developed and used by the business sector, such as *Lean Six Sigma, Total Quality Management,* and *Just-In-Time Logistics.* In an era of fiscal constraint, implementation of these practices is generally seen as a reinvestment of the "peace dividend" earned by our armed forces.

We should also recognize the value of reinvesting the "war dividend", or the knowledge and skills we have gained from the last decade, into the business institutions that make our society great. Decades of uncertainty and persistent conflict have forced the military to inculcate organizational flexibility and adaptability into its ranks. Faced with similar uncertainty, businesses could benefit from understanding the principles and practises that have proven successful in the military time and again.

One such concept that is ripe for use by our business leaders is Mission Command. This form of leadership and control has its roots in the decentralization of authority, the empowerment of subordinates, and the calculated risk-taking required in complex operations. These elements are as applicable to the business organization operating in today's competitive global market as they are to the military organization undertaking complex combat operations. The importance of providing the men and women of our organizations the values, flexibility, and trust to achieve the desired results transcends the public–private divide.

While the military has gained greatly from business practices over the years, it is good to see that, through books like this, the concepts and practices hard-won by the men and women of the military on the battlefield also have a place in today's boardrooms.

Lieutenant General David G. Perkins has spent over 30 years leading the men and women of the United States Army at almost every level of command. He employed the elements of Mission Command while leading troops over multiple tours in the Republic of Iraq and is now the officer responsible for the education and capability development of Mission Command across the US Army.

When a cold wind blew in (the dilemma of business leadership, one for all or all for one?)

A senior manager sits at his desk on a bright spring day, waiting for an e-mail. The tension in the office is palpable with concern and fear as today would be the day that individuals would find out whether they had been selected for redundancy.

Regardless of position, seniority or length of service, the whole company would be informed at the same time in the same way by e-mail. The office grew quiet as the time approached, everyone became obsessed with their mail inbox and a deep sickening feeling came over the manager. He knew that whatever news was brought to him many of his friends and colleagues would be distraught at the outcome; today would not be a good day at the office!

The e-mail arrived: individuals reacted in very different ways, some quietly carried on, others burst with emotion, crying and rushing from the office, some spent long times on the telephone to family and friends. Whether the news was good or bad everyone within the office was deeply affected by the events of the day. As the news spread across the office the inevitable questions were exchanged and some people immediately started to clear their desks, pack up and leave while others busied themselves with making alternative arrangements. The days that followed saw the inevitable deeply emotional goodbyes.

While the events that unfolded were extremely personal and emotional the corporate body kicked in with a well-oiled, professional, and impersonal methodology for managing the process.

The objective was to transit the spare capacity out of the business as quickly and efficiently as possible. A well-defined process of interviews was set in motion and methods of communication were quickly put in place so everyone understood where they stood.

The restructuring and redundancy program was a management process methodically applied in order to achieve maximum efficiency, a classic example of modern business management practice. The manager found himself in a dilemma, he had been among the numerous redundancies, however, he was torn between acting in his own self-interest (getting up, leaving the team, packing his belongings, and exploiting the best opportunities for his own betterment and future employment potential) or staying and looking after those individuals who had also been given bad news and leading those members of his team who needed to carry on and work through to build a new social and economic environment beyond the process.

The manager made the difficult decision to stay and work through his redundancy in order to provide support, guidance, and advice for all members of his team.

This manager also happened to be a reservist army officer who felt passionately that his position was more than a transactional relationship between himself and his colleagues; it carried personal responsibility and commitment that went beyond the boundaries of the organizational relationship. The individual's actions during this difficult period added weight, credibility, and experience to his leadership qualities, his character had been tested and he had emerged from this experience with great credit. If individuals are defined by their actions then this was a test that helped shape the individual. However, this person's actions were the exception rather than the rule.

The seeds we sow

Modern business management practises are becoming increasingly reliant on control through transactional relationships. The principle prescribes that individuals will work and accept direction in return for an agreed reward and that this transaction is the basis for the relationship between the business leader and the follower and it forms a key foundation principle for capitalism. In turn capitalism has been a successful economic model that has played a significant role in shaping modern society and has defined key relationships across the globalized environment. Although the interpretation of capitalism has varied throughout history and across geography the central principles of private ownership and transactional exchange have provided the basis for motivation, competition, and continuous advancement. The rise of the industrial model and the subsequent growth of the professional business manager have created a new breed of highly-rewarded employees that do not own the means of production but control the transactional relationship between the employees and the business (the means of production). The need for specialized business management has grown along with the size and complexity of business organizations. The role and relationship between management and ownership has significantly shifted in recent times from direct ownership to the managerial control of assets (means of production). This relationship has been underpinned by the requirement to maximize all the available assets of the business. As people are a critical attribute of any business's capability the requirement for business managers to be effective, dynamic, and transformational leaders is an essential requirement for success.

The utilization of transactional management has proved to be an effective method of controlling management processes providing that the output of the relationship has wider benefits for the whole organization. However, the increasing reliance on transactional relationships alone has promoted self-centered leadership behaviors that encouraged outputs to be focused on the benefits of an increasingly small number of individuals often at the expense of the wider community. This phenomenon has been crystallized in academic agency theory research. The emergence of the ever-increasing number of management evaluation methods ranging from independent audits, corporate structures (non-executive boards, remuneration committees, and board evaluation consultants), and shareholder restrictions (enforced voting restriction on specific corporate action, limiting direct board decision-making latitude) all illustrate the growing concern of this corporate phenomenon.

A cursory glance at the statistics on pay differentials makes worrying reading. Within a five-year period, the pay gap between the average CEO compared to the average operative in the UK has supposedly jumped from 18:1 to 180:1. Certain statistics emerging from the US make for even more worrying reading where a 1480:1 differential is even greater than that of Russia which stands at about as 1400:1!

Although the pay gap is staggering the recent report "What are we paying for? Exploring executive pay and performance" by The High Pay Commission stated that;

> There is rarely a link between directors' incentives and the way a company performs. In the past 10 years, the average annual bonus for FTSE 350 directors went up by 187 per cent and the average year-end share price declined by 71 per cent.   (Hargreaves, 2001, p. 4)

Increasingly, the criteria for success are narrowing to a single financial return as the key measurement. This singular definition is driving business managers to become increasingly concerned with short-term rewards.

Box 1.1   The retail king

An owner manager, who did not want to be identified, reported an enticing inspirational story to his employees. It was that of teamwork, all working together towards a great future and all owning part of the business. Employee ownership never came to be but the language of motivational leadership was in great supply. The owner manager in question was certainly smart. He owned/ran a chain of popular retail outlets. His skills of being disciplined over costs were legendary. His listening to the customer was as equally acute. He regularly replenished the stock in his stores with the sorts of items customers wanted. In fact, on certain occasions, queues formed outside his stores to be early purchasers of a new product range. Also, being well connected with the press and media, the individual had an acute sense of branding. On top of all that, he paid his people below average market rate but lured them with the promise of being part of the business. Quietly, the individual bought out his partners. The occasional grumblings of "shady deals and being put under pressure to sell from my partner of all people" filtered through. At its peak, the owner manager sold the business to a competitor. The new owners slashed the cost base and used their acquisition as a channel to market their own products as well. Many of the original staff and management were surplus to requirements and were made redundant.

Angry with what they viewed as betrayal, both staff and management confronted their owner/boss shortly after the announcement of the sell.

"We worked hard!"
"We built the business."
"We never asked for more because you promised we would share in this successful venture."
"You did not just let us down, you deliberately deceived us."

These were some of the comments that just gushed out within moments of having started the meeting. The considerably enriched but embattled former owner manager listened for just a short while and then commented, "I am an investor. I took the risks, but I also gave you jobs. Investors grow businesses and sell them."

Leaving the audience with the feeling "Are you so dumb that you couldn't see that." He finished with, "I paid you to work hard. You could have left at any time."

One of the more vociferous in the audience shouted out, "If all we are to you are things, a commodity, why did you then raise our hopes and make us feel that we were part of your team?"

The owner-manager shrugged and left the room followed by a stream of abuse, interestingly mainly from the women. The particular store in which the meeting was held was located in an area of high unemployment where for many families the women were the bread winners.

Wealth generation over the past 20 years has been increasingly concentrated on a small number of individuals (less than 1 per cent of the population) with an increasingly larger percentage of available wealth being controlled by the financial elite. This phenomenon has been repeated over the globalized economy, "The richest 10 per cent of adults accounted for 85 per cent of assets. The bottom 50 per cent of the world's adults owned barely 1 per cent of global wealth" (Davies, Sandstrom, Shorrocks, and Wolff, 2006, p. 26).

Furthermore, a report by Martin Shankleman (2008) of the BBC illustrated the dispersal of monetary power in the UK (one of the world's richest countries) through access to disposable income when he reported that "the top fifth of households have 42% of total disposable income, and the bottom fifth just 7%."

The drive to realize the maximum financial return has driven individuals to consider the short-term personal benefits of the transactional process as a valid method of participation in, and justification for, management action and leadership authority. Business leadership is becoming focused on self-advancement and self-interest as some of the large corporate remuneration packages in the midst of the international financial crisis clearly illustrate.

This kind of leadership does not create a sustainable environment where the mass of society will continue to support this model of social order. The signs of friction, dissent, and disquiet at this inequality are beginning to emerge – democracy is not necessarily aligned to a global capitalist model if organizational leadership does not reflect the wider societal requirements for advancement and betterment. History teaches us that great civilizations that promote the concentration of power, wealth, and self-advancement into the hands of the few at the expense of the majority are destined for destruction.

It has been argued by many academics and practitioners that any organization that relies on the ability of a key person at the top of the organization is living dangerously. Indeed, research by Probst and Raisch (2005) highlighted that a major cause of decline in an organization can be found in it being run by a top executive who has too much power. Often this can be spotted when a single person holds a number of key positions at the same time, for example, Chairman, CEO, president, and possibly a major shareholder. Probst and Raisch noted, in their research that explored the contributory factors associated with organizational failure, that:

> Almost without exception blessed with a charismatic and self-confident personality, the leaders used their autocratic position to pursue aggressive and visionary goals. The press, shareholders, and analysts praised initial successes with increasing rapture. These leaders were the "superhero" Bernie Ebbers at WorldCom, the "genius" Jean-Marie Messier at Vivendi and the "godfather" Percy Barnevik at ABB. Surrounded by followers, they indulged in increasingly excessive conduct. Tyco's CEO Kozlowski was called the "Roman emperor" and Ahold's CEO Cees van der Hoeven, "the Dutch Napoleon." Prior research has identified success, media praise, self-importance, and weak board vigilance as key sources of CEO hubris. In this research, CEO hubris has been related to large acquisition premiums and weak performance. CEO hubris, manifested as exaggerated pride or self-confidence, played a substantial role in the failure of the examined burnout companies.   (2005, p. 94)

Such lessons can be further extrapolated to help explain the underlying reasons for the failure of nations states such as the former Soviet Union or indeed the fall of the Roman Empire.

Box 1.2   Let me tell you what happened at Lehman Brothers

I (Andrew) was asked to make a presentation at an Economist Conference in the late autumn 2010. The theme was the role and responsibility of boards, especially at times of crisis. The results of my global study strongly identified that boards are intimately aware of the challenges facing their organization but that they find it difficult to discuss sensitive issues. One of the "elephants in the room" was the global financial crisis (GFC) and how many board directors were warned of the GFC years before. My research also pointed to the great volume of near to liquid capital in the City (£500 billion) and on Wall Street ($3.7 trillion) waiting to be invested in similar short-term transactional deals that would, in a few years, lead to an ever more catastrophic GFC. The audience was speechless.

My presentation over, I was leaving the hall when an old friend congratulated me on the speech.

"You have explained what has been bugging me for the last . . . months," my friend continued, "I was hired by Lehman Brothers to run a leadership program. It went well. One evening in the bar, one of the more senior Lehman guys told me, 'We are going to go bankrupt in about 18 months.' I asked him why – his response 'we are peddling shit and the market knows it and it is all going to fall apart in about 18 months.'"
"Why do it?" my friend asked the Lehman guy.
"Because of the money."
"So what are you going to do?"
"Nothing because of the money we are going to make."
"So what are you going to do?" asked my friend.
"In 18 months get a job with another bank to put all this right," was the response.

The contrasting approach to business: the military experience

In contrast to business the military has been involved in complex operations for the past 20 years. Arguably, the British military were ill prepared for the recent Middle East interventions, the challenges of the complexity and ambiguity of these operations have forced the military to re-examine the basis of how they lead and manage in these emerging contexts. Understanding the long-term nature of intervention, building trust, and changing social action begins with an alignment of needs, desires, and joint outcomes. In turn this builds trust and promotes co-operation and engagement. The tactical actions of the battlefield have far reaching consequences that cannot be predetermined by detailed planning, nor can a transactional relationship either inspire your own forces or engage the wider population, it must be a shared model based on understandable values that resonate across the cultural divide, justifies actions, and builds consensus as to a desired end state.

The dichotomy between the approach of Western business management action and the enforced lessons that have emerged from the military engaged in intense and testing operations have manifested two very different leadership, management, and social approaches. In the past military and business practise have shared a great deal and continue to be inextricably linked through social requirements. This book examines the diverging practices of these organizational models and provides a framework from which critical analysis and insight can be drawn and applied in today's context.

Going back to the basics to remain competitive

The British military had based many operational assumptions from their drawn out engagements in Northern Ireland and Yugoslavia. Both of these charted the changing face of military operations from a high-intensity kinetic conflict through to a civil war insurgency campaign. In effect this delineated the battlefield and made military decisions difficult to decouple from societal leadership. Military intervention had become the catalyst for state building and social restructuring. This new environment presented numerous challenges, compounded by the growth of consumer technologies that enabled global real-time information exchange. The military struggles to meet the demands of the increasingly rapidly emerging context. Operational decisions that were based on plans drawn on old assumptions became obsolete, awkward, and inappropriate as ground forces appeared unable to cope with the dynamics of these protracted operations. This forced the military to rethink their approach, they went back to basics, rediscovered the requirements of sustainable operations and promoted the empowerment of values based on real-time decision making. This allowed the troops to feel their way into the societal construct of the battlefield in order to judge right from wrong, apply appropriate behaviors, and make key decisions based on how they understood the values and standards that sustain a vibrant and energized society.

The term "doing the right thing" became a touchstone in order to capture the values-based approach that the military adopted. The concept is predicated on shared values and relies on the whole organization understanding, buying into, and promoting those values in all that they do. This is not a prescriptive application of abstract values, it is the promotion of values that individuals identify with and feel are worthy and necessary for society to exist. Values become the foundations from which individuals can make decisions in ambiguous and complex circumstances, they provide a foundation framework from which action can be justified and outcomes supported, not from the basis of retrospective analysis but from an honest and transparent evaluation of the events as they emerge.

The reliance on values-based leadership and empowerment of decision making throughout the organization contrasts sharply with the current business management practise where power and key decision making is becoming increasingly concentrated into a smaller number of individuals.

In contrast, business practice has promoted a transactional basis for managing and leading social groups. The concept that individuals can be controlled through financial rewards has gained significant traction in the past 50 years and has now spawned a new social and economic elite that appear content to control individuals through this approach. However, is this sustainable, will the wider society continue to agree that this is the best model upon which to base social order, or will the new challenges of the global environment bring new values and new perspectives? Already questions are being asked of the old social structure with increasing signs of social friction, the lessons of the past and the present are there to be seen: it is a question of whether we heed the warning signs.

Military leadership beyond the battlefield!

The military model has stood the test of time providing the guiding principles for some of the country's greatest leaders. The British military model is worthy of greater investigation in order to understand the essential components that combine to give an effective operational output that is appropriate for the military context. A closer examination of the complex combination can shed valuable light as to the key requirements of effective leadership for the business environment and the future challenges facing the global economy. The military model illustrates how leadership and command (authority) are fused together to provide robust management outputs that deliver high performance; it highlights the importance of trust and empowered risk-taking as a source of competitive advantage. The development of these capabilities is the responsibility of the leader. These shape the requirements of selection of the leader's qualities, capabilities, and beliefs.

> What does it mean "when you gaze long into an abyss the abyss also gazes into you"? (Nietzsche, 1886, Aphorism 146)

The first century BCE scholar Publilius Syrus once wrote: "anyone can hold the helm when the sea is calm" and in this simple sentence Publilius captured the essence of leadership; it is not a management function but rather a function when management process can no longer cope with the context. Leaders need to be effective at making decisions and guiding others through ambiguity, complexity, and volatility, not necessarily providing the answers but by giving clear direction and providing the foundation from which the answers will emerge. The ever increasing pace of global volatility illustrates that the sea is not calm and effective leadership of our organizations within the global society is becoming a critical concern.

The rise and fall of civilizations have witnessed great advancements in social order, knowledge, and enlightenment. However, these advancements have often been forged in the crucible of conflict. Since the beginning of time man has been engaged in a permanent struggle between ideologies, economies, and nation states. While the science of war has changed considerably throughout the ages the nature of the human condition and the fundamental dynamics of man engaged in conflict has not, the fears, hopes, aspirations, and motivations are almost unchanged.

It is the intensity of conflict that brings forth the very best and very worst of the human condition. The most destructive state of existence has often been the catalyst for new ideas and innovation. War and the individuals who have been engaged in the art of war have defined our understanding of many wider social influences such as leadership, decision making, and management. The nature of the human condition has never been so critically examined and understood as when the consequences of failure are so extreme. Today we understand conflict in a much wider spectrum from interstate high intensity war through to individual insurgence and pressure group factions, these smaller self-directed actions are often termed as terrorism. However, the ability of these groups to organize and deliver effect has been transformed in recent times. Whether conflict is manifested through interstate action or through individual acts of terrorism it is the intensity that the individual feels that creates the catalyst for change and transformation.

Throughout the pages of history there are many examples of great civilizations that have enjoyed military success. It has often been at the point of a spear that concepts of democracy, education, and religion have been spread and in turn have established new sources of intellectual capital. Some have captured the essence of their military exploits in official histories or unofficial documentation. It is perhaps understandable that the unprecedented level of conflict witnessed in the past 100 years has provided a rich source of information and analysis of the nature of individuals engaged in conflict. The twentieth century witnessed the transformation of conflict from interstate limited war to the application of industrialized methods in two world conflicts. The size and scale of the human endeavor of these wars have touched all aspects of our lives and the nature of society across the world. They have shaped the world in a way that no conflicts have done before.

The influence of the British Army

The British military is acknowledged as one of the best military forces in the world. Although many of the key observations, theories, and practices described in this book are shared across the three services (Navy, Army, Air Force) the key focus is the British Army involved in operational deployments and high intensity conflict, peace support operations (PSO), and the ever increasing wide range of various other hybrid operational contexts. The

British military has enjoyed success in many different kinds of operations, achieved great victories, and recovered from crushing defeats. Its resilience, durability, robustness, flexibility, and incredible operational performance often in the face of overwhelmingly unfavorable odds, ranging from Trafalgar and Waterloo, through to Korea, Northern Ireland, Bosnia, and the Falklands has given it a unique quality and one that is worthy of wider investigation.

The British Army has selected and developed leaders, evolved a resilient culture, and produced operational flexibility and organizational agility that are highly effective. The military has operated with a high degree of success in challenging and diverse circumstances. These enduring capabilities could provide real transformational opportunities for the business world to help meet the challenges and achieve success in an ever increasingly turbulent business environment. Aspects of this have long been understood within the business literature and this can be evidenced within the academic textbooks on marketing strategy where the war analogies are abundant with strategies such as encirclement, guerrilla, frontal attack, and flanking being taught on most business studies courses. As the military has faced new challenges and have re-examined their methodologies they have emerged with a greater focus on core organizational values. This approach has wider implications and offers valuable lessons for the modern business practitioner.

The British Army's approach

Few organizations have spent as much time understanding the dynamics of leadership as have the British military. This thinking has crystallized key concepts that are applicable to the business executive operating in the current environment. The British military place a great deal of importance on team performance with the aim being to unlock the wider potential of the organization. This requires a holistic self-sacrificing approach by the leader (at multiple levels through the organization) – qualities that are rooted deep within the psychological identity of the individual. Organizations that value collective performance may well find the values-based leadership approach an important asset in delivering enhanced operational capability. Figure 1.1

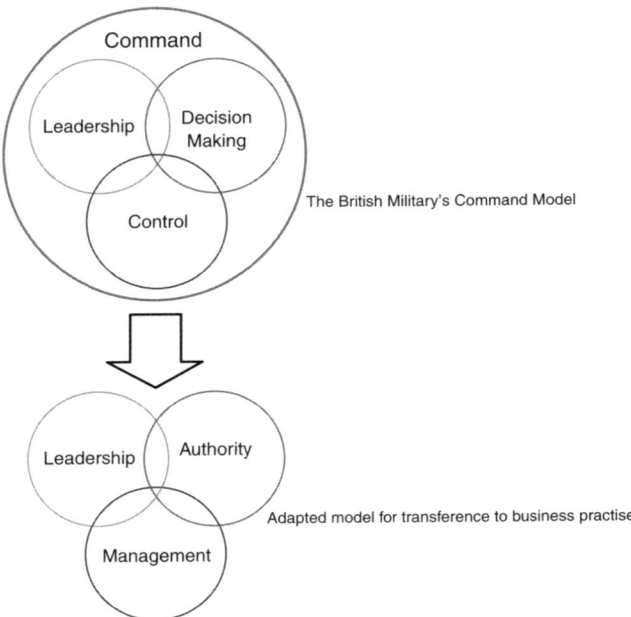

Figure 1.1 The adapted British Army's Leadership and Command Model for the business practitioner

Source: Presentation to Advanced Command and Staff Course (Reserves) by Ivan Yardley in 2011.

illustrates the key components of the British Army's Command Model; it forms the basis from which the military understand the dynamic requirements of effective leadership that are then translated into a practical context. The model has been adapted to illustrate the foundation terminology for the business practitioner. The British Army describes leadership from a grounded perspective, placing leadership within a practical context.

The thinking behind the British military leadership approach

A huge amount has been written regarding leadership, most management books give an increasingly large amount of space to the importance of leadership. It is important to note that the military "Command Model" describes leadership within a command paradigm reflecting the strict boundaries of the specific context in which the military operates. This integrates the function of leadership in a decision-making/control process that provides effective outcomes. The military approach and the adapted model require further explanation in order to provide foundational understanding and to identify the relevance for business transference.

For the purpose of Figure 1.1 we will define leadership as the quality that allows a person to attract followers – to get people to do things that they otherwise would not. These "pixie dust qualities" have attracted a huge amount of interest in recent times with many leadership theories such as the behavioral, situational, role, prescriptive, transactional, and transformational theories having evolved to meet the needs of the dynamic business environment. However, the British Army has remained relatively constant in their leadership model and although they spend a considerable amount of time selecting and developing leaders it is very much a grounded experienced-based approach that has served them well for many years.[1]

Controlling chaos, herding cats the military way

Although the military's leadership philosophy has evolved over time the same cannot be said for its attitude to control. For many years the British military viewed the management of complexity and volatility from a traditional perspective. The military, like so many organizations today, were committed to comprehensive analysis and detailed planning in an attempt to "second guess" every possible outcome. The commitment to control of the context led to an ever increasingly rigid approach that was dramatically challenged by the more flexible and agile German tactical response demonstrated in the latter stages of World War I and throughout World War II. It could be argued that although the Germans lost World War II the German Army performed to a consistently high tactical standard even in the face of overwhelming numerical and material pressure through the combined actions of the allies. The Germans' ability to rethink organizational design to make a more efficient response to emerging situations was largely forced from the necessity of their increasingly desperate situation. However, it should also be recognized that the German Army had laid the groundwork through its Officer and Senior Non-commissioned Officer (NCO) training prior to and during World War II. Even in the final year of World War II a German NCO received more comprehensive training than a British Officer. This level of selection, preparation, training, and mentoring provided the foundation for the operational performance of the German Army.

Feeling the way through the danger, making the critical decisions

The experiences of World War II combined with the pressures of the Cold War made the military rethink their Command Model. The rethink led to the formal adoption of an empowered and devolved decision-making process known as "Mission Command." This decision-making process accepted that control of the context was impossible and a source of competitive advantage could be achieved through shorter decision-making loops that retained

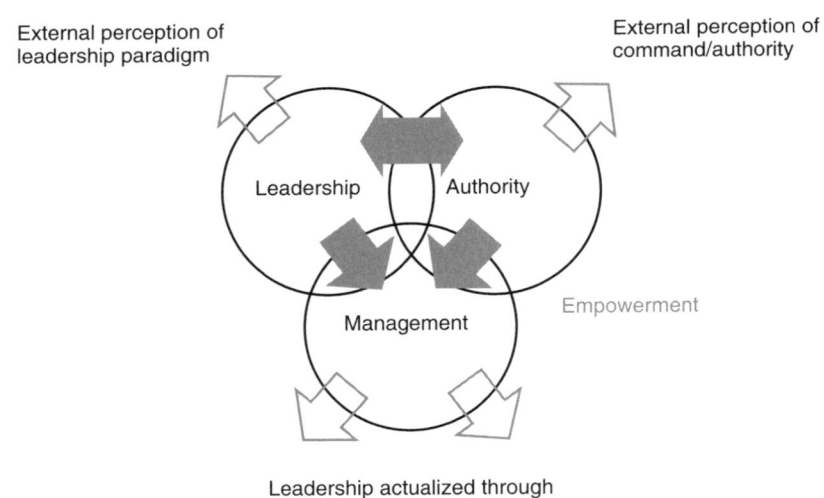

Figure 1.2 Leadership and Command Model for the business practitioner

Source: Presentation to Advanced Command and Staff Course (Reserves) by Ivan Yardley in 2011.

focus through military processes which provided effective control throughout the chaotic phenomena of conflict. The mission command decision-making process is described in detail later.

Business also suffers from constrained resources, operating restrictions, and an increasingly competitive and complex global operating environment. For most organizations a strategic plan that was predicated on the assumption of overwhelming resources and capability would demonstrate flawed thinking and inefficient and costly practices.

The simplified model shown in Figure 1.2 removes the formal command paradigm and explores the constitute components of the military approach from a business perspective.

Authority, a signature of legitimate power

As mentioned previously the military's understanding of leadership is encapsulated within the dynamic context captured in Figure 1.1, where the leader is supported through a command paradigm most easily identified by the imposition of "rank." The British Army uses a simple system of rank to impose a command structure; this structure legitimizes the use of power on behalf of the wider organization. The command foundation can be swapped for any organizational position or title such as Managing Director, Doctor, Judge, or Police Officer. Each title carries a number of assumptions regarding the role, experience, and authority that the individual is expected to embody. The preconceived expectation must be validated through experience in order to maintain legitimacy of role. In short the command position legitimizes the leader's action and vests organizational authority in their decisions. However, these decisions and actions must be in keeping with the preconceived expectations for the command paradigm to be maintained. As an example, if a policeman is seen taking bribes his action is at odds with the expectations of the role. His actions have undermined the position of authority that is vested in the individual and the position. If the problem becomes widespread the reputation and legitimacy of the organization can be undermined and questioned by the society that has vested authority in the role. Recently the actions of some top executives regarding pay and remuneration have led to the wider society questioning the ethics and legiti-macy of these individuals.

When I (Ivan) was working for a large corporate organization a new senior director was appointed from outside the organization. The new senior director had very little understanding of the cul-ture or the individuals he was to manage. I was amazed to find that he had no interest in finding out about what people did, their experiences, or what they had to offer. It became clear that he had a defined agenda and that this was centered on his own profile and self-advancement. His plan was simple, reorganize his port-folio, save money through outsourcing and shedding capability, and then move on as quickly as he could before the ramifications of his decisions could be felt at the operational level of the busi-ness. During a series of meetings I became increasingly despon-dent about his attitude, neither the interests of the business or the welfare of the staff appeared to concern him. He was ambivalent to the mantra of "doing the right thing" by anyone except for himself. As part of his plan he implemented a number of highly divisive policies and practises and soon morale dropped and subordinates began to question the legitimacy of management. The actions of this senior leader also eroded the belief people had in the organization itself. If the organization could vest so much decision-making power in this individual and support his man-agement practises then the ethical foundations of the business, its concern for its staff, and sense of community were also tainted by the actions of this individual. The toxic nature of the individual's actions had wider consequences; many subordinates who were not directly involved in this process witnessed the effects on col-leagues and were amazed at management's lack of concern. Soon members of staff began to "drag their feet," had little appetite for carrying out management practices and a dysfunctional and disruptive culture began to develop. Disappointingly it became the justification that the director needed to make the changes that he proposed. It was a situation of his own making, one that cost the business a great deal of money, disaffected staff (many of whom left), and eroded the reputation of the business in the eyes of the staff. The only winner was the individual. He left a trail of destruction that is still to be cleaned up many years after his action. Unfortunately, far too many senior managers adopt this approach because they seem unwilling or incapable of effective leadership and sound management to create real value for the business and their subordinates.

A window on the organizational soul

The third element of the model is that of management. It is important to separate leadership (the qualities of the individual to get people to follow them) and management, which is the ordering and allocation of resources. Management is the process through which most people will experience leadership. It is the day-to-day decision-making within the management function where individuals gain the experience and awareness of the kind of leaders they have, the culture of the organization, and a sense of its values. Combined, these provide a legitimacy and motivation for action. Separating the definitions of leadership, authority (command), and the function of management allows the British Army to crystallize the essential components of each function. It is worth remembering that context provides a dynamic and fluid environment where an individual can be both a leader and a follower; the process of management can be exercised through a personal action or by processes enshrined in the organization. The development of staff manuals provides a foundation upon which management can base its actions but the exercising of power is a combination of leadership and authority and the legitimacy of a decision will stand or fall on the leader's discretion and ethical evaluation by the wider community. The function of leadership and the process of being a follower is dynamic and interchangeable, especially within a multi-organizational context.

Get them young: the military's approach to selecting leaders

The British Army selects their leaders at a comparatively young age. This can be between 21 to 26 years of age, although often individuals have been prepared through long attendance at organizations such as the Officer University Training Corp (OUTC) or Army Cadets prior to attending selection at the Army Officers Selection Board (AOSB) for a short 4-day residential assessment.

All candidates go through a number of assessments that range from a command task, essay writing, and cognitive tests through to presentations and discussions with the aim of identifying leadership potential. Business utilizes a range of selection methodologies in attempting to produce a robust selection program, although it must be noted that most commercial organizations recruit workers and not leaders at this stage. Some companies employ an increasingly sophisticated range of selection methodologies for the selection of senior staff where leadership becomes an essential criterion of role function. Many corporate organizations use external consultants to conduct the leadership selection process while others utilize the services of specially trained internal staff. Many corporate selection programs depend on a combination of isometric tests that attempt to identify characteristics and working patterns (trait theory) in an attempt to identify "natural leadership qualities". However, they often ignore two essential elements for successful selection, namely the culture of the organization they will lead and the tasks they will be expected to perform. Both of these dynamics can have a profound effect on the success or otherwise of the selection of the organization's leadership.

A foot in both camps

I (Ivan) have been fortunate in that I have undergone both military and business selection programs for leadership. It struck me that the military conducted a number of exercises that were aligned with the core functions of the role that I would be conducting while my business selection tests were broader and less specific. The business selection processes focused on the identification of generic leadership qualities with the expectation that a good leader could be successfully utilized in any context. This contrasted with the military's view which was more specific. They wanted leaders who would thrive in their environment and people who would be good at leading in the military context.

Cart and horse: getting it right from the beginning

The British Army first selects their leaders based on leadership potential then invests time and effort in training them in the practical techniques to be effective leaders. This process is in stark contrast to the business world where an individual is identified and selected for promotion often due to technical excellence. The identification of business talent narrows the focus to individual, rather than team, performance. Although understandable this method of selection identifies individuals who are focused on their own performance rather than helping to promote the wider team success. The British Army highlights the importance of team performance and that it is the responsibility of the leader to get the very best from the team and it therefore makes sense to select individuals who demonstrate this quality from the beginning.

The British Army look for and attract individuals who are motivated to serve others, individuals who feel it is their role to inspire and lead others to perform tasks and achieve things that otherwise they would not. This kind of transformational perspective of leadership is akin to a catalyst igniting the potential in others. It is therefore important that these values are shared by all officers within the military and are well understood by all members of the forces. This simple process of selecting leaders allows for greater understanding within the military community of the role of officers and why they are so important in collective team and organizational performance.

The benefits of this approach are self-evident, however, it can also be restrictive; the military find it very difficult to bring external senior staff into the organization. As the nature of operations change and the drive for organizational efficiencies becomes even more challenging the need for deep-rooted industrial specialists increases. The process of recruitment of senior specialists has begun but work on their integration will need to be continued, modified, and adapted to produce the organizational agility required for the future operating context.

Remind me of the role of the leader again

The role of the military leader is not that of a technical expert (although a high level of professional competence is expected in order to maintain legitimate authority) but of a facilitator and catalyst for change. This may be through innovation, intervention, or identification of talent and all of these critical roles require direct action, effective decision making, and the preparedness to accept risk and promote team performance. The military leader must be an individual that maintains high levels of integrity in order to build and maintain trust and this is different from being popular or even liked. Individuals must understand the role, what motivated the leader, their standards and values. These must be transparent and shared in order for the team to understand the social context, to feel comfortable with what is expected of each of them, and to have the confidence in the leader to perform those tasks.

The basic foundation of this form of leadership is inherently a shared-values framework; a set of values that are deeply held and personal to the individual. The leader's values inform their decision making but, more importantly, they guide the individual beyond their training, experience of cognitive capability and in time of complexity and volatility. They provide the support to effective decision making and appropriate leadership behaviors even when the situation is highly stressed and ambiguous. Having shared individual and organizational values also provides a common understanding even when the role of leader and follower is interchangeable.

Values guide decisions when experience or training becomes limited

The British Army has been involved in a number of increasingly complex operations. The operations have often proved to be challenging with rapidly emerging situations that have stretched individuals who have been faced with decisions for which their training and experience have not provided a route-map solution. At these times individuals must rely on their values, what they believe are the right things to do, and they must understand their actions in the wider context and be prepared to defend their decisions. The role of the leader is to set the moral framework, through direction and action. By living the values of the organization each individual is left in no doubt as to what they should do in times of ambiguity. The British Army has a

The Army's Values	The Army's Standards
Selfless Commitment	Lawful
Courage	Appropriate behavior
Discipline	Total professionalism
Integrity	Application
Respect for others	

Figure 1.3 The values and standards of the British Army

Source: Taken from *The Values and Standards of the British Army*, January 2008.

set of organizational values, shown in Figure 1.3, that are shared across the whole organization. These values are at the heart of the leader selection program and are critical to effective leadership practise. The interpretation and articulation of organizational values will vary from individual to individual. However, they sit within culturally recognized parameters of acceptable organizational practice.

Each of the values and standards are expanded to give the audience a practical context for application and therefore identify their relevance and purpose. It is interesting to note that when the British military has deviated from one or more of these values it has incurred strategic consequences even if the deviation was a relatively minor or tactical point. With the advancements of information technology and a new generation of social content generation the rapid assimilation of tactical events can have far reaching consequences. Many businesses also have values charters but a key difference lies in selection and training. The values businesses often aspire to are rationalized, imported criteria: a wish list of values that the organization hopes their staff will exhibit. However, few select their staff based on their values, and it is important that values-based behavior is demonstrated by management practices and leadership action. Values-based behavior needs to be rewarded and nurtured in order for it to become embedded within the culture of the organization.

The dawn of these capabilities has not changed the nature of conflict but has provided greater complexities within the management of context. The number of unprogrammed variables that can now be identified, recorded, and published over the World Wide Web (WWW), each with the potential for strategic consequences has inevitably meant that a greater responsibility is placed on the individual who will make the decision, often under extreme conditions, to act or not to act. It is the recognition that the environment is complex and volatile and that events lie beyond our control that has driven the military to accept an empowered approach. This system of command and control is called "Mission Command" but it is leadership that makes it work.

Walking the walk and talking the talk

Authority carries responsibility, a responsibility to act in a way that followers believe you should do. The interdependency between the authority position and the person who fills the post acting in an appropriate manor is critical in maintaining legitimacy. For an authority position to be established and maintained it is important that the post and the level of power that is exercised through that position is perceived as being legitimate.

Legitimacy involves many different facets but although the authority paradigm can be established by the organization only the individual who holds the post can maintain that legitimacy of authority. It is essential that the individuals who hold and exercise power on behalf of the organization have the leadership qualities that are required to maintain these positions. Values-based leadership provides the framework within which a leader will make decisions even in times of uncertainty and ambiguity that are congruent with the expectations of the authority paradigm.

Sustainability, balance, and flexibility

Leadership is exercised through an authority paradigm which may be organizationally bestowed (such as the military selection and promotion of officers as organizational leaders who are identified by rank) or it may be socially given when a leader is self-selected from their peer group. Leadership is a dynamic state; many individuals can manifest qualities of leadership if the context is right, however, only those who are perceived to obtain legitimacy will be able to execute decisions effectively. Ensuring that organizations attract and select the right kind of leaders, both from an external market and from within the organization, for the right level of authority is critical in developing a robust and sustainable leadership function that is capable of dynamically managing the organization beyond simple transactional situations. The executive power that is invested in the individual and realized through the decision-making they perform on behalf of the organization is benchmarked against the values of the organization. Therefore, when the British Army describes their actions within the phraseology of "doing the right thing" it is a description of acting in accordance of the values and standards of the organization.

Legitimacy can be eroded over time at an individual, organizational, and even national level, for example, the US in the conflict that resulted from its intervention in Vietnam. The US won almost all its tactical engagements in Vietnam but they failed to make the case for the legitimacy for their actions and soon the military lost the support of both the indigenous population and the people of the US. As the war became perceived as illegitimate it became more unpopular and the US faced strategic defeat.

Box 1.3   Legitimacy

Legitimacy is not only the preserve of military organizations. In the financial crisis of the early twenty-first century large corporations and specifically the banking industry shouldered much of the blame. These organizations continued to pay large executive bonuses even when the general population (who financed these organizations through tax payer's contributions) faced huge cuts and raised taxation in order to foot the bill. This failure to understand the general mood of the wider community produced anger as the bank's actions were seen as unjustifiable and lacking legitimacy. Just like the US in Vietnam the banks may have won the tactical victory but lost the strategic campaign.

Measuring outputs through management action

Management is the process of organizing resources; this can involve a number of functions and combines people, physical and intangible resources. The function of management is often described through processes that define activity. Organizations evolve standard management approaches that are defined through rules and procedures; these provide a standardized approach to a specific problem. Management aims to produce greater efficiency and effectiveness within an organizational context.

The style of management and the outputs of the management functions are reflections of the leadership philosophy within the organization. Management positions and titles organizationally signpost the position of leadership and signify levels of power that can be legitimately exercised by the holder of the position. Therefore, the combination of leadership and command provides the foundation of management; if the foundations are weak then the management outputs may become inconsistent or inappropriate especially under times of pressure.

Analyzing management methods, processes and standards can give valuable insight as to the type of leadership and values the organization may have. Aligning these foundations with the organizational aims and the wider context are fundamental to delivering sustainable organizational performance. Alignment of the individual, the group, and the organization's culture, management practises and values are critical because they are mutually supportive concepts that need to resonate across all aspects of the organizational experience.

The British Army has analyzed the framework for the "Command Model." This has enabled the military to select appropriate leaders, invest authority and power in them, and train them to be effective managers. This structure provides a robust understanding of leadership within an organizational context.

The framework of leadership, command, and management needs to be applied in context and individual parameters need to be placed around each theme to, as an example, determine the "right kind of leader" style or approach. In the same way the British Army has faced a changing context with greater variables, tasks, and challenges that stretch the training, selection, and resources of the organization. Today's businesses are also facing a similar stretch within their own operational context and finding it ever more important to appreciate the facilitative role of the leader. The military understand that much of the deep-rooted technical knowledge of a specific solution will rest within the organizational mass, empowering and engaging the wider capabilities of the organization – important for realizing successful outcomes.

Leadership needs to be appropriate for the role and function that the organization demands of its leadership. This may sound simple, but while the British Army requires leaders who can function in a highly volatile and complex environment, this does not mean that all organizations require the same nature of leadership.

Adaptation, rationalization, and implementation, you choose!

The British military's Command Model (1995) provides a useful framework from which an organization can produce functional outputs. The model has been rationalized in order to crystallize activity for a specific context, Figure 1.4 illustrates the conceptual approach to provide the theoretical foundation upon which adaptation can be applied.

This approach recognizes the importance of values as being critical in an individual's decision making especially in times of uncertainty and ambiguity. The model still requires the individual to have the intellectual capacity, communication skills, and wider attributes of a leader but places greater emphasis on the relevance of values both of the individual and the organization. Aligning individual, organizational, and cultural values provides a foundation from which the leader must exercise their decision-making authority. Acting in accordance with those values provides legitimacy for action and promotes a leadership philosophy that is sustainable as it acts in accordance with the wider organizational beliefs and benefits.

Utilizing values gives a usable handrail for dealing with complexity, volatility, and ambiguity where decision-making cannot

Figure 1.4   Values-based leadership, a model for effective leadership

be based solely on an analytical, process-driven methodology of deduction, as is often the case in the "real" world. Accepting these dynamics offers a source of competitive advantage for those organizations that are able and willing to seize the initiative and promote positive action on behalf of the wider organization. This kind of leadership transparency promotes trust through leadership action, personality traits (mutual understanding bounded by shared beliefs and values), and shared experiences.

This adapted model promotes the use of intuition and instinct, not through a cavalier approach to risk, but because of the inability to rationalize all variables within the operational context. It accepts risk and acknowledges that failure is a possibility but it mitigates the longer term dangers of decision failure by placing the decision outputs within a shared values context. Individuals can understand why a decision has been made, analyze and scrutinize the actions of their leaders, and understand why a particular action has been taken.

Good or bad decisions are often measured with the benefit of hindsight; this retrospective analysis can be dangerous if it unduly promotes reliance on sterile analysis of a dynamic context. This thinking will provide an over reliance on predictable linear implementation plans and inhibit empowered decision making providing an organization that is constrained by centralized decision-making based on old data.

Without trust you have nothing

> *The team that trusts – their leader and each other – is more likely to be successful.* (Mike Krzyzewski, 2011)

As all leaders, at any level within an organization, know developing high organizational performance requires high levels of trust. Improving performance requires individuals to accept and take risks. The leader needs to empower others, develop individual competencies and team capabilities; this requires the leader to take risks, to place trust in others. By demonstrating that the leader trusts others, a sense of responsibility and commitment is developed but the leader must accept that some individuals will not perform to the standards expected or perhaps they will not develop the competencies and capabilities that the leader believes they have the capacity to achieve. These failures and setbacks must be understood within the wider context and the leader must accept that some individuals will not make the journey within the team. It is an important function of leadership that every individual understands the commitment of the leader and that standards must be set and achieved. It should never be a surprise to an individual that they have not made the grade; if it is, then the leader has failed to communicate with and mentor the individual. Trust can be built or eroded during training and shared experiences where the leader and follower are working together to produce outputs. This interaction builds experience and understanding that forms the basis of trust within a relationship.

Developing and sustaining trust is a vital component of employing a risk-taking management methodology. Empowering individuals is more than the diffusion of organizational power; it's creating a culture of responsibility acceptance. Individuals have to understand that they have a responsibility to act or perhaps not to act and to make decisions without referring to the leader. Empowerment will be discussed later, however, it is an important point that without high levels of individual and organizational trust empowerment and risk-taking cannot be sustained.

Trusting leaders and trustworthy leadership

The development of trust is the responsibility of the leader and is maintained through the function of effective management. As discussed previously the values of the leader are critical as when an individual is performing under stress they will often make decisions based on their innermost beliefs. Their values framework is the foundation from which they will determine the decisions they make. Combining quality leadership and legitimate authority aid in the maintenance of organizational and individual trust. Maintaining the balance of leadership legitimacy is determined through the decisions that are made and the policies and processes that are adopted. Transparency and effective communications enable the wider community of practitioners to understand and evaluate the decisions that are made. When decisions are confused or inconsistent with the accepted values of the organization then the leadership legitimacy will be challenged.

Trust is developed more quickly and sustained within teams that share common values and culture; this binds the team together through a common acceptance of purpose and values. Although this observation would seem obvious it may have wider implications for selecting teams for high performance. It should be a significant consideration when organizations are selecting and managing teams. It is interesting to note that companies that are trusted by consumers often have strong internal values and cultures that are recognized beyond the organizational boundaries.

During a Masters in Business Administration (MBA) course the group work was driven by a technique called "action learning." This centered on a group of students who were self-directed. From this they determined the research program from which to learn and develop their own response. The group was not directed or supervised because the aim was to develop the skills required for learning and independent application and thus produce an individual who could operate independently and not rely on old taught knowledge but was free to continuously learn new information and methodologies. The groups were self-selecting and each year of the course individuals could be voted in or out of the year group. This slightly uncomfortable process gave great insight into team dynamics and the last year of the course was particularly intense and the group that I (Ivan) observed took the deliberate decision to self-select like individuals. They were all male, broadly the same age, and had agreed the general rules of the group before selection took place. This process of pre-selection was slightly shocking but it produced a very task oriented, directive team that worked effectively and efficiently. The lack of diversity in the group undoubtedly affected the depth of the decision-making and perhaps the quality, however, the group were the most efficient group in the year and all passed the MBA with good grades. Depending on the task and the role of the group, diversity is not always a desirable status quo, sometimes teams that have very similar backgrounds and views can quickly and efficiently work together to produce high quality work under pressure. This familiarity provides a foundation of trust through shared goals and experiences without having to forge new common ground.

Implications for identification, selection, and training of leadership/senior management

The British Army has developed a grounded approach to selection and development of leaders within the framework of an evolving dynamic organizational context. The role of the military in the current operational environment is evolving and becoming more involved and interwoven within a number of wider parameters. The military has responded to the lessons of recent complex interventions with the adoption of a wider understanding of the operational context and this is incorporated in the "comprehensive approach." Figure 1.5 illustrates the key attributes of the Comprehensive Approach and highlights the foundations of a society.

The development of the Comprehensive Approach attempts to capture the wider elements of a society that need to be addressed within the context of a military intervention. This framework

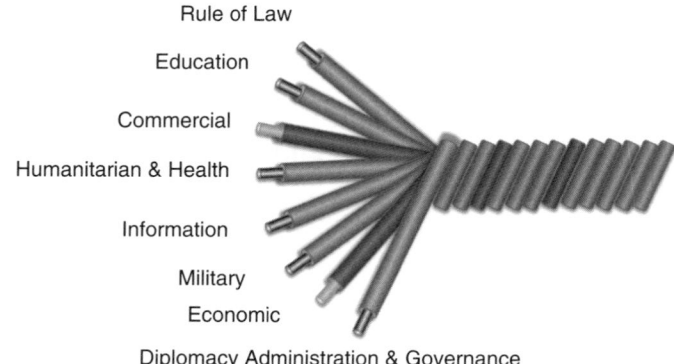

Rule of Law
Education
Commercial
Humanitarian & Health
Information
Military
Economic
Diplomacy Administration & Governance

Figure 1.5   The Comprehensive Approach represents the constituents of a society

Source: *The Comprehensive Approach*, Joint Discussion Notes 4/05, Jan 2006.

forces the planners to consider each component of a society and requires the operational plan to address the other authorities and resources that are required to achieve a successful outcome. The increased pace of globalization has forced the world to take note of individual conflicts that have the potential for contagion within the wider global economy. These interventions are more involved, longer term, and sustaining in nature than previous interventions. The comprehensive approach has been extremely useful in capturing the wider lessons of the current military interventions and it has also highlighted a number of challenges for the military, not least that far greater "stretch" is required in their leaders. This is necessary to lead other organizations through influence, persuasion and, at times, coercion in order to provide a comprehensive successful outcome. The key issue that has emerged from this analysis is the selection of leaders that are appropriate for the organization and deliver effective leadership in the relevant context. Perhaps business should focus on the values and characteristics of leaders rather than solely on their technical competency.

Many United Nations (UN) missions now last in excess of 10 or 15 years with some extending to 20 years or more. Although the military are not involved in all aspects of the comprehensive approach they have a critical change role, as it is often a military response that is the catalyst for change. The military leader has a wider remit than the comparatively narrow focus of command: they are now involved in the persuasive nature of negotiations with other organizations that hold the resources and capabilities that will determine the success of the intervention. Many military officers find the transition from a command paradigm to a negotiated, persuasive leadership approach difficult conceptually; this friction was expressed by Lieutenant General Sir John Kiszely as:

> The force commander is operating in a largely civilian and multinational environment, with a large proportion of his job involving leadership by persuasion and management. This is not dissimilar to the job of the chief executive officer (CEO) of a large multinational corporation. Time spent understudying such a CEO might be time well spent for potential force commanders. Furthermore, a CEO who was also a reservist officer might be particularly well qualified as a force commander.   (Kiszely and Royal United Services Institute for Defence and Security Studies, 2008, p. 25)

Lieutenant General Sir John Kiszely's comments capture the concern and the recognition of the increased complexity of the comprehensive approach and perhaps insightfully recognizes the military's lack of experience in this central role within the comprehensive methodology. As the military has addressed the wider context of the expanding operation envelope of the global economy so too must business. The recent economic crisis illustrated the vulnerability of the global economy but many of the individual organizations that operate within the global market still fail to understand the wider implications of their actions.

Box 1.4   Understanding the wider implications (Barclays)

On September 7, 2010 Barclays Bank announced its new business head would be Bob Diamond. Mr Diamond is a highly successful investment banker with, supposedly almost no knowledge of retail banking; his pay is estimated to be £1.35 million per year with an annual bonus of £3.37

million (*Financial Times*, September 7, 2010). In the midst of the worst financial crisis the world has witnessed and at a time when the main banks are increasingly being blamed for the crisis Barclays bank decided to make this critical appointment with a disregard for its wider consequences. Barclays are not alone, most of the main high street banks have continued to pursue a high-bonus, high-reward policy for their staff with what appears to be little regard for the long-term implications for banking within the global economy and what affect will this have on Western economic and social policy.

Although the context in which the military operates is changing and therefore the demands placed on the military are evolving the nature of what the military does, its core function, the nature of conflict, and the requirements placed on those individuals who can lead in this uncertain environment has not. The military first select individuals who demonstrate leadership qualities; these are based on values that are translated into decisions and performance that lead others to perform as high-quality teams.

The leader must be trained, mentored, and exposed to risk in order to prepare the individual for effective operational performance. Non-military organizations may benefit from the military's approach. Within the commercial world this would require a critical examination of selection and development of leadership.

Summary

The military utilize a simple framework the "Command Model" which provides a framework from which leadership can be effectively exercised. The military has optimized their approach to provide effective outputs based on the military context, although this context has become more complex in recent times the basic functional model is still valid for current requirements. The comprehensive approach has placed new challenges on the military model that will require less prescriptive outputs and a deeper exploration of the "stretch capability" of the military model. Selection of leaders based on leadership qualities (based on values rather than on technical management competencies) enables the development of a high-quality leadership philosophy that provides an appropriate response to a complex and volatile context that is increasingly difficult to control. There is no such thing as a universal "right leadership model." However, there is an appropriate leadership model that requires a sympathetic management methodology that is engaged and responsive to the operational context of the organization.

Accepting the unpredictable nature of context provides the opportunity for competitive advantage to be achieved through more agile and empowered leadership responses. This requires co-operation and engagement of the wider organization in order to leverage the full capability of the intellectual and physical assets of the organization.

The engagement of the "hearts and minds" of the organization requires quality leadership that is inspiring and engaging, committing individuals to work as a team, to subdue their own ambitions for the benefit of the wider community. This kind of leadership is transformational and engaging.

Organizational leadership requires understanding of the competitive environment in order to benchmark performance and the ability to perform better than the competition, to innovate and inspire continuous renewal, which provides the cutting edge of the organization. Quality leadership provides the foundation for sustainable organizational performance, it needs to be built on values and attributes that resonate across the organization and inspire the individuals who serve it.

Although the nature of military combat is very different from the business environment, competition, complexity, and volatility are contextual dynamics that most business practitioners would fully identify with. Selecting the right kind of leaders that are capable of leading in this dynamic context is the starting point but providing the methodology and culture in order to support an empowered limited risk-taking management methodology is just as important. The British military has taken many years of trial and error to develop this approach; it has stood the test of time and is grounded in the toughest and most demanding of environments. The key concepts now need to be adopted and adapted in order to deliver the same dynamic, sustainable competitive advantage in today's turbulent global economic landscape.

Note

1. The AOSB was established in 1943 and has, fundamentally, employed the same process for selection with only relatively minor amendments.

CHAPTER 2

The changing face of leadership in the global context

The history of civilization has witnessed the rise and fall of great societies. These have evolved complex and sophisticated internal social structures that have required leaders to direct, organize, and allocate activity and resources. As societies evolve they develop new organizational structures that place new demands on social leadership. In the past, societies have been defined by distinct social boundaries with clear identities and shared values. Today the interconnected markets are blurring the edges of the old social structures and asking new questions of leadership within a complex and dynamic global context.

The evolution of society has spurred many great technological advances; some of the most important advances have facilitated transformational knowledge exchange over the full spectrum from the individual through to societies themselves. The step change in the individual's ability to capture and exchange knowledge has witnessed exponential growth and advancement, although this chapter will deal with three such examples of knowledge exchange it is important to note that innovation and social structures are continuously evolving.

The exchange of knowledge has transformed society in both size and complexity with concepts of social participation, democracy, and ethics emerging as fundamental binding principles. However, these concepts have also raised new questions for social leadership, legitimacy, authority, ethical behavior, centralization of power, and decision-making; all fragile concepts that are continuously reviewed for relevance and utility in the emerging structures.

As the old Western economic model gives way to new emerging global influences we need to question whether our management practises are still appropriate for this globalized society. The previous chapter outlined the challenges facing management based on transactional relationships alone, suggesting that this form of organizational control is in danger of promoting self-centered and short-term leadership traits that no longer serve the wider organizational context.

Economic globalization has been facilitated by the development of technology that enables better communication and knowledge exchange; this in turn has impacted on social structures and society's aspirations. These developments are not new, throughout history developments in technology have allowed society to capture and share knowledge that has changed the requirements of social leadership. The events of the Middle East have witnessed social protests that have demanded radical political and economic reforms, however, it is not the demands but rather the way they have been organized and exploited that demand greater interrogation. The use of technology has allowed individuals to self-organize and prosecute diverging aims by groups that are willing to collaborate on specific issues in order to achieve different goals. These transient social structures are not defined by distinct bounded characteristics but rather through ideology, leadership is transient and emerging in nature and proves to be challenging for old social structures.

These challenges are not dissimilar to the changing nature of military operations. The past 20 years have witnessed a radical change in how military intervention is used in the wider exploitation of foreign policy. Military forces have been required to meet the challenges of enemies that are not defined by organizations or figurehead leadership but rather by ideology, organized through technology, social and knowledge exchange that combined produces a significant asymmetric challenge to military success. The military has been forced to re-examine the lessons of the past and apply sound leadership in order to engage the wider organization to meet this challenge, producing an agile operational force that is capable of responding appropriately to a dynamic and complex threat within a volatile and unfamiliar environment.

The examination of leadership development of the past provides critical insight as to how it may respond to future challenges, the military has been required to face these challenges, to cope with changing social dynamics, and produce an effective organizational response. Perhaps the lessons of current military operations provide valuable insight as to how a business operating in the global economy may provide effective leadership.

The current business environment and the impact on leadership thinking and theory

As societies have evolved new organizational designs have emerged, for example, the manufacturing business model during the industrial revolution. These models placed new demands on leadership that in turn promoted the practise of management and gave rise to the professional business manager.

The rise of the professional business manager is well documented and evidenced by the proliferation of business schools throughout the world. Leadership forms a critical cornerstone of the business executive's professional education. Understanding the changing context is fundamental to developing business practices that are appropriate for current organizational requirements.

Businesses are redefining their own organizational boundaries with the growth in outsourcing and strategic partnering blurring the edges of the traditional organization. Business managers need to be effective at managing in ambiguous and uncertain environments while maintaining an organizational aim. Examining British military practises provides valuable insight as to how another organization manages this dilemma. The British military has defined and implemented leadership and management practises in extreme environments providing a robust methodology that can be adapted to meet the challenges often found in commercial organizations. This thinking has wider implications for the identification, selection, and training of leaders, defining management activity and understanding the nature of the connected concepts of leadership, authority, and management.

The demands and role of the leader is a dynamic and evolutionary process, as social structures evolve so too will the requirements of leadership. However, the current economic model has led to a confused tension between the functional role of management and the importance of leadership. It is this tension that has given rise to the questionable practices of executive remuneration and city bonus packages. In order to understand the current environment and to draw some conclusions as to the future it is important to understand how we have arrived at our current position.

The historical roots of business organizational design

The role of leadership and the emerging nature of management practices are grounded within an historical context. It is important to understand the interconnected relationship between cause and effect in order to appreciate the significance of new technologies, emerging social organizational forms, and the implications for leadership and management practice in the future.

From the beginning man has huddled together around communal fires and found solace within a social structure. These early communities improved opportunities for sustaining life as they provided higher levels of protection, sustenance, education, and resulted in a more rapid development of social infrastructure than would otherwise have been the case. The more successful communities exhibited characteristics of a crude social structure with aspects of task specialization, skills transfer, and the establishment of acceptable and unacceptable behaviors and as a consequence they grew larger. The great city states of the classic Greek period of 500 BCE represented a sophisticated society where large numbers of individuals lived together, sharing common laws, education, systems of governance, and many of the other social structures that are recognized today as being fundamental core constituents of a society. Although these city states were large for the period they are miniscule by comparison with today's standards. The growth of social structures is limited by a number of factors such as access to food. (The early city states of Greece were limited by the amount of food that could be grown locally or imported by comparatively limited logistic capabilities.) As societies grew they came into contact, and sometimes conflict with other societies. Much can be learnt from the challenges these early societies faced, but perhaps the most noted examples of their capabilities can be witnessed when they were mobilized for war.

Changing nature of business organizational form and the implications for business leadership

Study the past if you would define the future. (Confucius, 551 BCE–479 BCE)

Much of modern business practise and management theory can be traced to key events that had a direct or indirect influence on social and organizational leadership. In order to understand and identify these key events a brief examination of the historical timeline is helpful. Social structures have evolved throughout history; a short appraisal of developments within the UK will illustrate the transformation that was taking place across many societies and continents at the time. Figure 2.1 illustrates a brief historical timeline of the UK.

All societies need to be able to defend themselves. Competition for resources has always been fiercely contested and the more successful societies throughout history have also had successful military forces. These forces were utilized to gain control or access to resources that allowed their society to grow and become dominant in a region. Social structures and organizational methodologies can be identified in the classic armies of the time. From the early classic period through to the industrial revolution, not only were armies the largest and most sophisticated logistical and social organizational forms of the period but they were often well documented. Classical armies (700 BCE to 500 CE) varied dramatically in size with the largest professional army being that of the later Roman Republic numbering some 400,000 men (Marcus Aurelius 121–180 CE) organized into legions of approximately 4,500 personnel. These forces were spread across an empire of over 50 million people. The ability of the Romans to dominate such a huge land mass and number of people reflected the comparative levels of organizational ability. The conquered countries of the Roman Empire lacked the ability to organize sufficient critical mass to disrupt the well-oiled administrative and military machine of the Roman Empire for

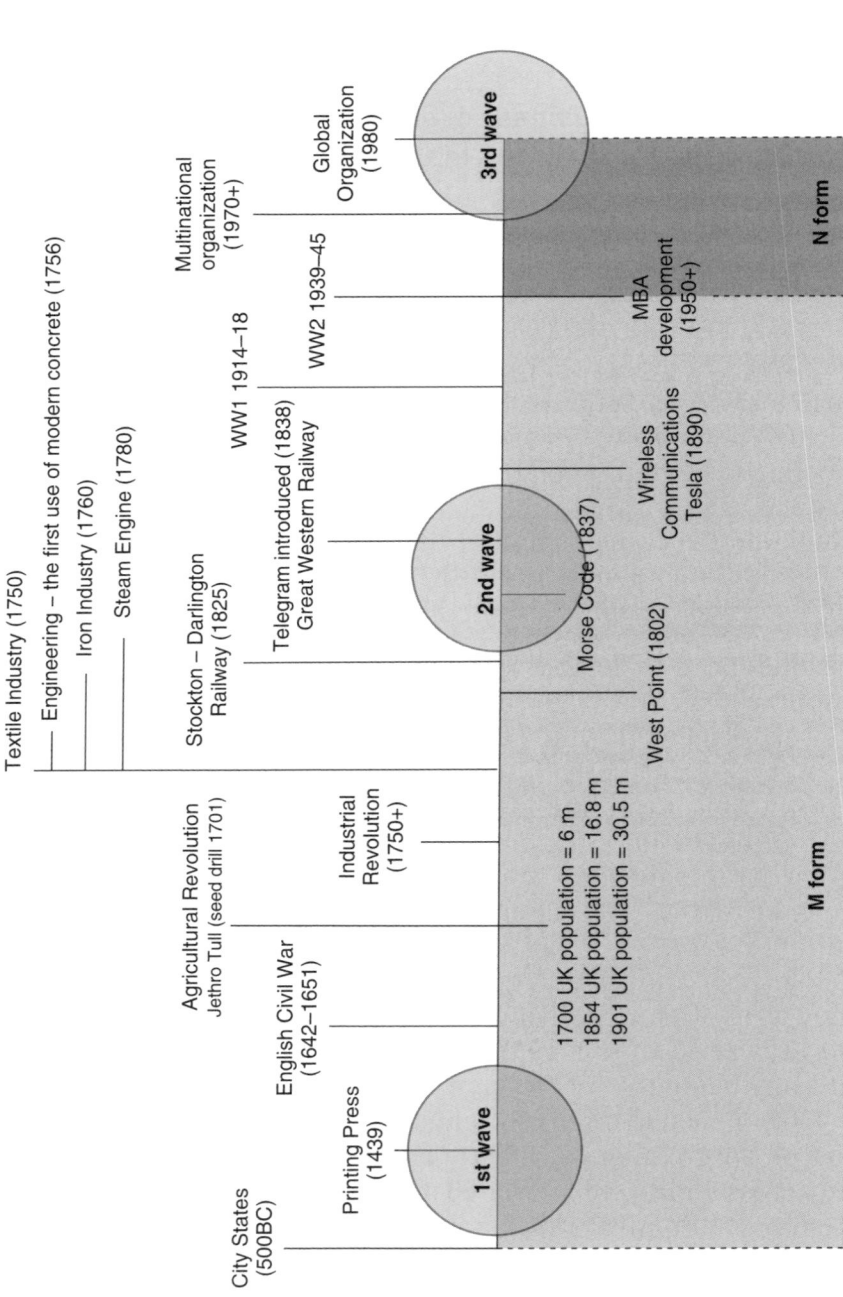

Figure 2.1 Historical events that shaped social context and the impact of knowledge exchange on social leadership

Source: Ivan Yardley (2003) presentation to Advanced Command and Staff Course.

almost 400 years. The model of the Roman Army can clearly identify the development of the classic "M" form organizations which eventually became the dominant organizational design for both the state and commercial organizations alike. (Figure 2.2 illustrates the basic M form organizational design from the early

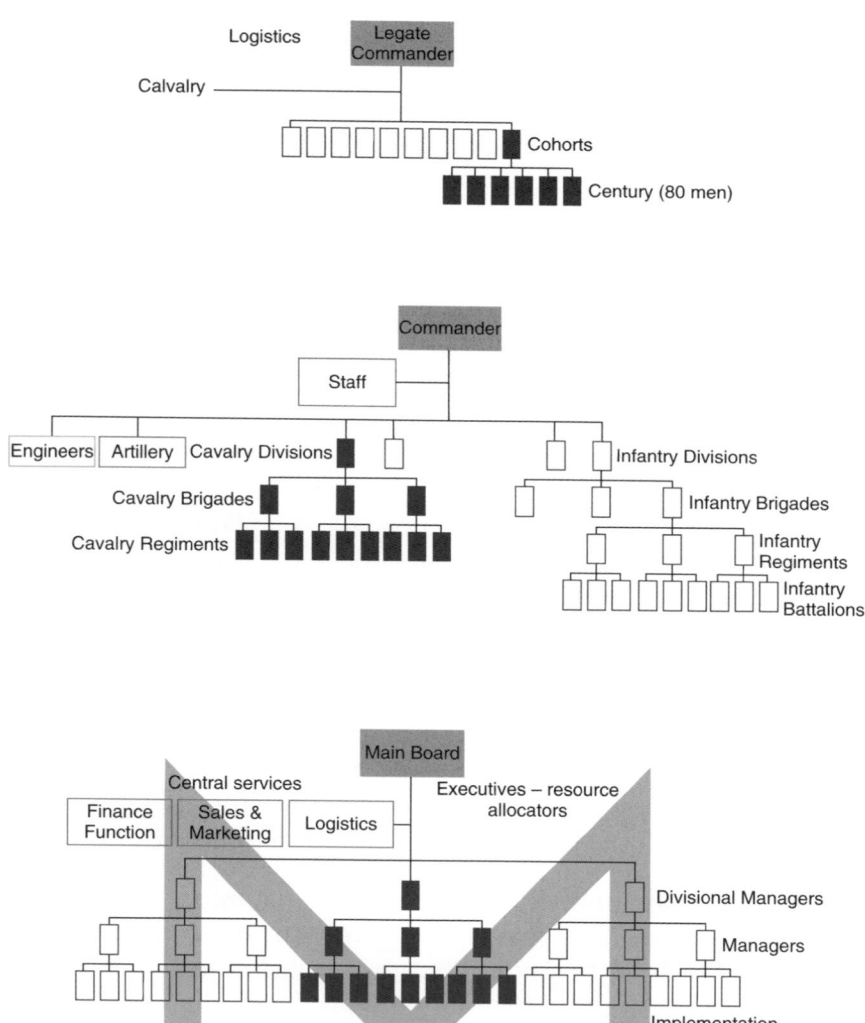

Figure 2.2 The evolution of the M form organizational design, optimized for efficiency

Roman legions, handed down through successive military organization and manifested as the dominant organizational design for business.)

The M form, the basis of organizational management

The M form organization is structured for efficiency and provides a balance between centralized planning and decentralized control. As the name suggests the M form, or multidivisional organization, is organized into specializations and divisional structures that provide a framework for effective social control. The M form may be oriented towards geography, markets, or functional specialization but the structure allows the centre to drive management performance and allocate resources more efficiently than would be possible with an unstructured approach. This system of management and control can still be clearly identified in most organizations today and has provided the foundation on which much of our current management practices have been based. The M form is the accepted basis of organizational design that is utilized within large corporate structures today and the thinking behind it has been claimed by academic research groups in the 1920s and 1940s. However, its roots can clearly be identified in many military organizations throughout history. From the Roman legions of the Roman army through to the current organization of the modern British military the M form or multidivisional structure has been in constant use. World War II questioned the limitations of the classic M form structure; it was the German Army, driven by the need to maximize efficiency that gave birth to a new way of organizing and allocating resources, as will be discussed later in this chapter.

The Romans abandoned Britain as an occupied territory in around 400 CE. This act of retrenchment signaled the decline of the Roman Empire and the onset of a period now termed the Dark Ages. During this period British society returned to a less sophisticated social model where many towns declined in size and returned to a subsistence rural economy, which dominated social life in Britain for the next 1,000 years. However, the legacy of the Roman occupation could still be witnessed through the comprehensive road building program that linked important parts of Britain providing an essential communications and trade infrastructure much of which still exists today.

The first wave of knowledge exchange begins!

In 1440 the German Johannes Gutenberg developed the printing press. This provided the foundation for knowledge exchange that would sweep across Europe providing the platform to capture and share knowledge across vast distances. Prior to the printing press, books were an exceptionally scarce commodity. Handwritten manuscripts were copied by ecclesiastical monks to provide the basis for knowledge capture. These manuscripts became the preserve of the ruling elite and provided the foundation for a highly centralized concentration of power. This can be witnessed in the creation of chained libraries such as at Winchester Cathedral where books were chained to tables in order to stop people from stealing them. With the development of the printing press new ideas could be documented, printed, and transported to other areas where the innovation could be replicated. With a growing availability of the written word a growth in literacy developed. This radically altered the balance and concentration of power from the state and religious organizations to the emerging middle and landowning upper classes.

Box 2.1 Gutenberg's printing press

Gutenberg invented the use of moveable type, a process that allowed the printer to construct the page of text from a block of type (originally the type was carved in wood and later individual letters were cast in lead). Mixing ink with oil allowed for smoother coverage and a better printing quality of individual pages. The original text varied between 38 and 42 lines of text on each page (the maximum number of characters the printer could construct within a printing plate). Gutenberg's printing press revolutionized the printing industry from single carved pages to pages that could be constructed quickly from individual letters and then reused to form new pages of text and this process dramatically reduced the time and cost of printing. Gutenberg's manuscripts such as his bibles would retail at about 30 florins (3 years wages for the average worker although considerably cheaper than the handwritten books of ecclesiastical monks each of which could take over a year to complete). The finished manuscripts were then hand illustrated in order to give the reader a rich visual experience of the book. The technology and knowledge of Gutenberg's printing press quickly spread across Europe and proved to be a significant catalyst for social and knowledge development.

More food, more people!

The dawn of the Agricultural Revolution was marked by the invention of the seed drill in 1701. This and subsequent advancements paved the way for a rapid increase in efficiency of food production and in turn a huge growth in population and life expectancy.

The growth in manpower provided the resources for the industrial revolution in 1750 and the development of centralized organizations based on the factory structure. These two transformational historical events were aided by the ability of individuals to share knowledge and innovation in a more effective manner than had previously been possible.

Industrialization of society: the masses need organizing

The industrial factory signaled the development of professional business management. These managers drew their experience from the largest organizational form of the time; the Army. However, in the early twentieth century the development of academic interest in professional management techniques began to emerge with the production of a series of papers and journals. F.W. Taylor's *Shop Management* (1903) and Henri Fayol's *Administration Industrielle et Générale* (1916) were among many others that discussed the merits of effective management.

Soon industrial organizations began to evolve and develop specializations that demanded more of the professional manager.

As businesses became bigger and more complex the military organizational form became less important as a universal organizational template. As the dominance of the military form began to wane, a growth in alternative management practises began to be crystallized in professional management journals, papers, and books. The Agricultural Revolution between the seventeenth century and the nineteenth century witnessed an explosive growth, in the UK's population, of over 500 per cent. This provided the human capital for the industrial revolution and the rise of the industrial corporate body bringing the population from the rural landscape into the ever-expanding conurbations. The scale and rate of population expansion created new challenges for organizational and social development that reverberated throughout the whole of society. The ensuing growth in size and complexity of organizational design began to present new challenges for leadership and management practise, however, the basic foundation of M form organizational thinking still remained the overwhelming dominant accepted basis for effective organizational design. During this period of rapid expansion the limitations of the M form were beginning to emerge but it would take cataclysmic events to challenge 3,000 years of accepted practise.

Transplantation of state to corporate leadership: a new religion

Box 2.2   The American Civil War

The American Civil War laid the basis for today's Anglo-American corporation. The war, supposedly driven by concern for civil rights, was in reality a bitter and deep conflict between two sets of American elites who held contrasting philosophies, the industrialists of the North and the agrarian landlords of the South. The war was financed through Abraham Lincoln's extensive reach into private capital through the issuing of bonds. Despite being challenged by treason, insurrection, and facing imminent bankruptcy, Lincoln not only won the war but also built the world's largest army and in so doing spawned an enormous industrial monstrosity, the steel industry. The construction of the continental rail system and the formation of the Federal Department of Agriculture followed. A new era of commercialization and commoditization began. Farm machinery and cheap tools became freely available across this broad landmass.

Yet, despite his enviable achievement, Lincoln feared what he had unleashed. In a letter to his confidante, Colonel William F. Elkins, Lincoln wrote,

> I see in the near future a crisis approaching that unnerves me and causes me to tremble for the safety of my country . . . corporations have been enthroned and an era of corruption in high places will follow, and the money power of the country will endeavor to prolong its reign by working upon the prejudices of the people until all wealth is aggregated in a few hands and the Republic is destroyed.   (President Abraham Lincoln, 21 November 1864)

Despite the City's and Wall Street's worship of shareholder value, Lincoln's fears have been realized. The US Founding Fathers' concern for preserving checks and balances has been undermined. Their view was that the American middle class would provide the necessary balance in society. One hundred and forty years later, the social, economic, and political influence of the entrepreneur has been swallowed up by the large corporations. Today's circumstances have been made even worse by the recent US Supreme Court ruling that corporations and unions can legally finance political parties. Reality today is that gaining an audience with a Senator or State Governor is directly determined by the size of the donation to their election fund.

At an Insead strategy and sustainability global conference (EABiS Colloquium) held in Paris on 27 and 28 October 2011, one eminent European captured the current state of affairs of the American nation by exclaiming "there is no corruption in the USA as it just been legalized!"

Today's state of affairs was not always the case as Lincoln strongly attempted to reverse the trend he initiated. He refused to repay the war bonds that financed the Civil War. Within a matter of days, he was assassinated. Some hundred years later, a similar fate befell President J.F. Kennedy. Drawing on his privilege to determine law through Presidential Orders, Kennedy introduced the "people's money" as the currency for the United States. Had his initiative been given a chance, America would no longer be debt ridden and the Federal Reserve Bank would likely have disappeared. Yet, hardly was the ink dry on Executive Order 11110, when Kennedy was dramatically shot in Dallas. The assassination investigation was brought to an abrupt end with the subsequent murder of Lee Harvey Oswald. A third, not so well known President, James Garfield, also met with a similar fate 80 years before Kennedy for his interference with the financial system of the American State.

A modern history of America shows how and why the corporation knows no boundaries. As with the birth of so many religions, that of the "Holy Corporate" has been as bloody as all of the rest.

A new challenge for business leadership, time and space: a new frontier!

In 1825 the opening of the first railway in the United Kingdom (Stockton to Darlington Railway) presented new challenges for organizational thinking. In comparison to the later Great Western Railway of 1838 the Stockton to Darlington Railway was comparatively small. However, it was the first commercial organization that was spread over a comparatively large geographical area. Prior to the invention of the railway industry most industrial organizations were located within a single geographical area and linked by a limited canal network; this allowed for the leadership model to remain constant. Like armies of the day commercial organizations demanded the "model of leadership" to perform largely the same functions and in the same way. A leader could visit most of the organization within a single day, know the staff, talk directly to individuals, and impose his will through presence and personality so although many of the management practises had diverged the recognized method of leadership had not.

The creation of the railways made new demands on the leadership model. The creation of the railways made it feasible for organizations to operate with multiple sites serving different geographical regions, and as a result placed new demands on leadership. For example, in the new environment it was no longer feasible for leaders to be physically present in their organizations and engaging with staff personally. Standard processes and procedures began to dominate linear organizations, allowing for centralized control to be exercised through stringent and prescriptive management practises. The development of the US railways signaled the dependence on the military organizational form and new challenges for leadership. The US railways were organized on the "rule of three" which is a simple system and typically involved, by way of example, three functional work teams managed by a single manager, every three managers would be managed by a senior manager and every three senior managers would be managed by a director. The "rule of three" is believed to be the optimum span for effective management with five or six being seen as the very maximum number of individuals that can be managed. Most military organizations still use the rule of three as a guide to organizational structure. The railways adopted this system directly from the military along with official titles such as "officer" and "division." The railways were the largest non-military organization to wear a standard universal uniform, a phenomenon that would be repeated across many large industrial organizations of the twentieth century. The wearing of uniforms and the adoption of standardized management practises gave the increasingly mobile population assurance as to the quality and standard of products and services the organization provided. Brands and corporate identities replaced the need for intimate local knowledge or personal experience of a specific store or service desk. The personal item became replaced with a mass-produced one, and this would later be modified by mass-customization providing the individual with quality assurance and a sense of individual tailoring of needs.

The second wave of knowledge exchange evolves

The drive for real-time communications in order to manage effectively these emerging organizational forms led to the development of the telegraph. Soon telegraph wires grew along the side of railways and roads providing an effective network of real-time communications. This reduced the requirement for the individual to be present in order to lead the organization. The invention of the telegram signaled the second wave of knowledge exchange. This ability to transfer information across large distances impacted on how individuals, organizations, and even countries made decisions.

In 1890 Tesla invented wireless communications. By then the world had become a global trading network with vast amounts of trade being conducted via the sea. However, until Tesla invented wireless communications, there were very few methods of communicating effectively with ships once they had left port. Tesla's invention provided the opportunity for goods and services to be bought and sold, effectively traded and reassigned even when the goods were in transit. These forms of communication transformed the role of leadership within the commercial environment; the knee-jerk reaction was to place greater emphasis on the management process instead of the then socially unacceptable practise of individual empowerment.

It is worth noting that during this transformational period the new and emerging US began to develop their own professional military class of leaders. West Point was established in 1802 to provide the platform to develop the skills required to build America. The vast majority of military cadets were engineers, signalers and had other logistic skills. Graduates from West Point built many of the US's ports, roads, railways, and large infrastructure projects. Military leadership combined with technical knowledge and sound management practises provided the capability to build some of the largest civil engineering projects of the day.

The incremental industrial developments would come to a dramatic head with the outbreak of World War I. The class of the old imperial empires of Europe would galvanize the world's economies in the provision of material for the war effort. Industrialization and management practises would be put to the test in the most demanding environment. The scale and intensity of World War I would require new industrial practices to be imported into the military's war effort with industrial specialist and management knowledge being adopted to provide military effect. The course of the

War saw many technical and industrial innovations and witnessed a huge shift in social practises and aspirations. The German offensive of 1918 over-ran nearly all of the British first- and second-line supplies. However, it is a testimony to the growing professionalism of the industrial managerial class and industrial capabilities that most of these were replaced with a few short weeks.

World War II was the first industrial war where entire economies were transformed in order to provide mass production of war material. The drive for increased efficiency and innovation focused the managerial classes' efforts on improving organizational performance. The severe shortages of people and material facing the German Army forced a radical rethink of how valuable resources were allocated. The German Army pioneered a process of allocating resources around a task. This meant that transient organizations were formed to perform a specific mission; units were borrowed from across the military organization in order to produce force structures that were optimized to perform the designated role. These structures were broken up and reformed for the next task, this form of task organization required standardized ethos, command and control, and a shared philosophy that allowed for organizational commitment and unity of effort in order to be effective in such demanding circumstances. The demands of leading an unfamiliar structure placed greater emphasis on effective, intuitive, and innovative leadership. The role of a battle group commander is to give clear directions in ways that everyone can understand and enables them to work in a co-operative way to achieve the desired effect. This new organizational approach became known as the "N" form and provided a radical alternative from the established M form organizational design of the day. The N form reflects the network structures that can be created and then reformed or dissolved when their purpose has been served. The N form empowers frontline staff or participants within the network to make decisions and act within a shared context. Although the N form was utilized extensively within the military it has been adopted by non-military organizations including public, private, and not-for-profit sectors and has been facilitated by emerging technologies. Social networks provide an excellent foundation for developing N form capabilities. Figure 2.3 illustrates a typical N form organization although many can be far more complex. The implications for leadership are returned to later in this chapter.

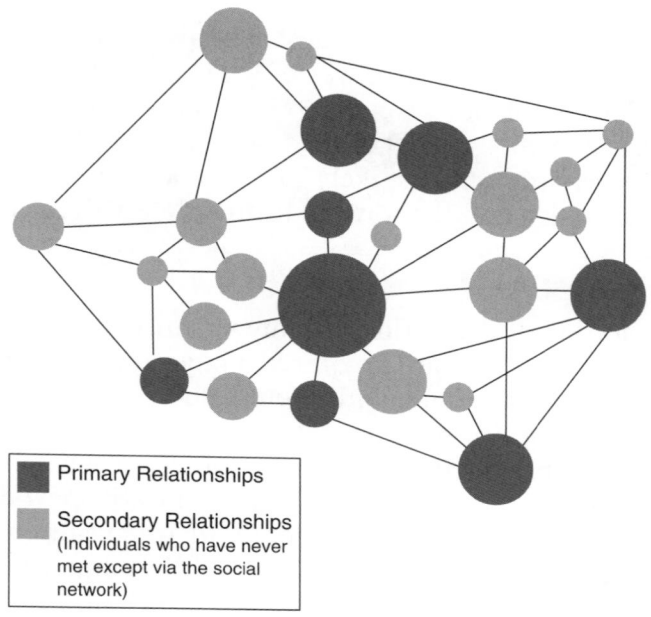

Figure 2.3 The N form organizational design

The combined effects of World War I and World War II had a profound impact on social expectations; the old structures of the pre-war years were replaced with an inclusive clamor for a country fit for heroes. The evolution of the UK welfare state represented a halfway house between capitalism and communism and recognized the equality and inclusive demands of the citizen.

Box 2.3   The Welfare State

The beginning of the welfare state in the UK can be traced to 1911 with the introduction of the National Insurance Contribution for all working citizens in order to provide basic unemployment and health service provision. In the UK further development of the welfare state under William Beveridge took place in 1942 and provided greater protection for people in need or in poverty. This eventually led to the creation of the National Health Service (NHS), which has become one of the world's largest organizations behind the Chinese Army, Indian Railways, WalMart, and the United State's Department of Defense. However, the restructuring that began in 2011 as part of the UK government's response to the economic crisis is likely to see fundamental changes both in the size and the way the future NHS will operate.

The devastation of the world economy and infrastructure caused by six years of World War II required a huge amount of post-war reconstruction. These demands were filled by a rapidly evolving private sector. Production switched from armaments to the production of bricks and machinery. Much of what had been learnt by management was quickly applied to the new demands of the peacetime economy. The underlying trend saw companies become bigger entities. Then international companies opened offices, production facilities, or logistic distribution centers in different countries but although these were multinational in terms of location they often had a center of mass in a single continent with shared time zones, trading, and fiscal regulations. The multinationals embraced globalization and companies had true global reach and complex economic and social structures that spanned time, culture, and social values. The global organization required different leadership and management traits that challenged the traditional organizational theories of the past.

The third wave of knowledge exchange

The invention and development of the Internet provided the communications framework from which social networks could self-organize and operate as a self-determining N form.

Box 2.4   Using the N Form (Wikileaks)

The use of N form organizational capability has come into focus through high profile cases such as Wikileaks. Towards the end of 2010 the Wikileaks website decided to publish thousands of US diplomatic records and cables that referred to a wide range of sensitive reports. The US administration tried desperately to prevent the publication of the material. First the US tried to prevent publication directly then by applying pressure to enabling components such as servers and funding lines. Each time the US administration attempted to close Wikileaks a new operating methodology self-evolved. Using the network enabled community of the Internet groups and individuals worked in self-organized communities to innovate new ways of publishing and sustaining Wikileaks. As the pressure increased the plight of Wikileaks drew more and more support from a wide community of practitioners who had never met but were prepared to work together in order to achieve a mutually shared goal. Wikileaks is a good example of an N form organization that is facilitated by the Internet and social networks.

Implications for leadership thinking

The previous section has illustrated the key events that have shaped our understanding of organizations and the requirements for effective leadership of those organizations. As organizational design evolved it placed new demands on leadership and management. From the early city states through to the first half of the twentieth century little had changed concerning leadership thinking; the great man theory dominated for over 3,000 years. However, with the end of World War II and the development of international and global organizations new leadership theories began to emerge. The intense interest in leadership has been fuelled by the creation of the Masters in Business Administration (MBA) as the gold standard for professional management training. Figure 2.4 illustrates the timeline for developments in key leadership theory.

MBA programs were originally designed to teach scientific management techniques to a growing professional business management class. In the late 1940s the MBA switched from providing courses primarily focused at the large public-sector bodies (created during the World Wars) to give greater emphasis

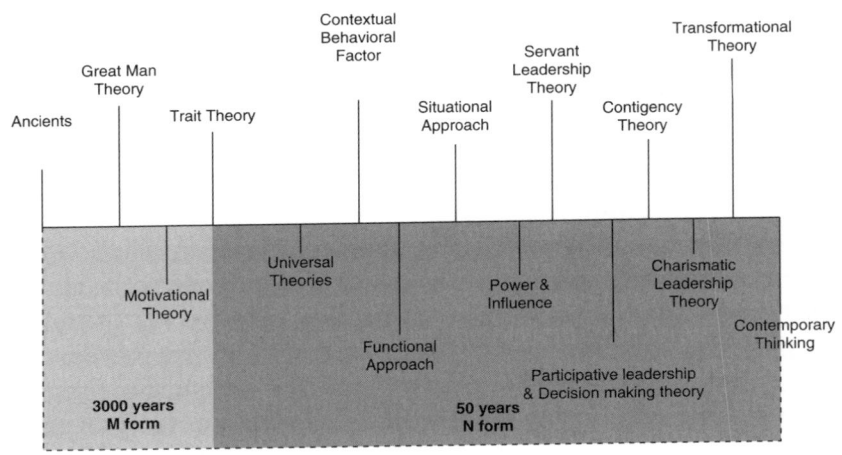

Figure 2.4 Charting the proliferation of leadership theory since World War II and the rise of the MBA

Source: Ivan Yardley (2011) presentation to Advanced Command and Staff Course.

on the private sector. The 1950s saw the MBA program exported from the US to Europe where the program soon enjoyed growing popularity among ambitious professional managers who wished to demonstrate their knowledge and capability by undertaking a formal management-training program. As the MBA program has evolved a great research emphasis has been placed on effective leadership for emerging organizational challenges. It is this research that has spurred so many new leadership theories. Although there have been many new insights and interesting hypotheses there are few leadership methodologies that are as well grounded in experience and carefully thought through as the one found in the British military.

One size fits all

The literature on leadership has evolved from the early days of the great man theory of the 1930s, which tended to be retrospective analysis of great leaders in order to identify common traits. In the 1940s and the 1950s leadership took on a behaviors focus with two dimensions being considered, namely behaviors that were task centered and behaviors that were relationship centered.

During the 1960s and 1970s the agenda changed yet again with the development of contingency theories and a move to consideration of the situation and its impact on the style and approach to leadership. Studies during the 1960s suggested that "servant leadership" was an appropriate leadership methodology for the then current business environment. Servant leadership theory suggests that leaders who aim to serve their followers will create greater engagement and commitment and as a consequence will develop higher levels of performance. More recently the search for understanding leadership in the emerging organizational context has suggested a values-based approach as an appropriate solution.

As the requirements of managing new organizational forms have become more demanding the evolution of leadership thinking has gathered pace. The British military has also been evolving and refining their leadership approach. The military benefit from the organization being drawn from a cultural group (the UK) who share common values. These are clearly articulated in the military publication *Values and Standards of the British Army* (British Army, 2008). Some have suggested that "servant leadership" thinking is based in a Christian perspective[1] of the world through the grounded development of social structures, laws, and accepted methods of behaviors in a culture where Christianity has dominated and directly influenced the development of the social construct. The accepted business management and leadership paradigm are largely based on a Western Christian business model; this borrows much of its ethical foundations from a Western perspective. However, as the British military are involved in more complex operations, which are more closely aligned with peacekeeping and the long-term view of society reconstruction, the use of the military as primary change agents has forced the military to consider a wider perspective. The intervention and management of a complex organization such as a nation state involves the consideration of the leadership style. The British military maintain their leadership paradigm but reconfigure the legitimacy or command paradigm. By changing the command authority it forces the leader to adopt a more facilitative and less coercive style of leadership. The intensity and complexity of the military context has driven this wider perspective and in so doing has revised the role of the leader in this multifaceted environment. The development of this comprehensive approach

(Chapter 1) provides the conceptual framework from which this modified style of leadership and management can be more effectively applied in order to achieve positive change outcomes.

The recognition of the critical role of values underpinning leadership action provides a foundation for ethical and sustainable leadership that can resonate across multiple decisions and changing contexts. It provides the unifying ethos to the wider organization and grounds the immediate requirements within a strategic philosophical approach.

The dynamic and emerging relationship between leadership, authority, and management is bounded by the changing nature of context. The historical timeline illustrates key events or innovations that allowed for greater knowledge sharing, this acted as a catalyst for social development manifesting in new organizational design and asking new questions of social leadership. The rise of Western economic and military power has ensured a dominance of Western values across much of today's global economy. These values are crystallized within the Christian perspective and permeate across all aspects of leadership, ethics, and accepted perception of legitimacy.

The growth of the global economy and the importance of the economic institution over the state have witnessed the transposing

Figure 2.5 Values-based leadership: a model for effective leadership

of the state and social values for those of management functional outputs. The revised managerial approach underpinned by transactional relationships is still to be tested as a sustainable approach for social order.

Figure 2.5 illustrates the interdependency of critical aspects of social cohesion that combine to provide the route map of effective leadership (as described in Chapter 1). As previously highlighted, leadership requires authority in order to legitimize executive decision making, this must be supported and sustained through perceived legitimacy of the leader (selection, attributes, behaviors, competence, experience, etc). However, the organization must be perceived as legitimate within the wider social construct, it needs to behave appropriately. Some obvious outward signs of accepted social standards can be found within the increased popularity of social responsibility charters underpinned by legal requirements of codes of conduct such as the financial credibility of an organization reflected within the annual audited accounts.

While the legal and social responsibility of an organization underpins the legitimacy and robustness of an organization it also demonstrates willingness to conform to social order through compliance with the legislation of that society. These functions of compliance and societal support are validated through behaviors of the organization and the individuals that lead those organizations. Increasingly, individuals and organizations are judged not only on the prescribed adherence to an interpretation of a legal framework but on a wider more inclusive and interpretive social, ethical, legitimate foundation. This more complex and personal framework must be deeply embedded within the values of the leader and reflected in the organizational policies and actions in order to be resilient and robust in the complex and volatile environment of today's global economy.

The demands of today and the implications for tomorrow's leaders

The nature of current operations and the changing nature of organizational capability required to achieve positive effects is clearly a strategic driver for developing adaptive leaders.

However, the growing evolution of the military's own organic capability continues to force a critical re-examination of effective leadership even within the confines of the British Military. The growth of Private Finance Initiatives (PFI), Public–Private Partnerships (PPP), and the outsourcing of services to private contractors (food, cleaning, maintenance whole fleet management of vehicles and logistics) changes the shape and culture of the British military: leaders now need to balance high-intensity conflict with detailed contract negotiations. The challenge is to select leaders who can adapt to the wide requirements of a large and complex organization. Lieutenant General Sir John Kiszely's statement (Chapter 1) identifies the use of reserve capabilities. By utilizing individuals who have a dual set of experiences he has found leaders who share the same fundamental values-set but through practical application have learnt to adapt their leadership management style effectively to fit desired outcomes.

Does the world share the same values?

The shared nature of values leadership provides a powerful unifying framework for developing inclusive leadership, however, not all cultures share the same precise values framework. The variety of values and how they combine to define legitimacy has profound implications for establishing and maintaining a global leadership approach. In Afghanistan, the British military has grappled with the complexities of introducing democracy with the long-term complex objective of rebuilding a state that has been reduced to medieval conditions. This has provided leadership challenges that are continuously being reviewed in order to provide workable solutions for this emerging context.

The development of self-determining social N form networks has wider implications for managing complex organizational contexts where the overriding desire is to restrict, define, and manage the organizational context in order to apply scientific analysis and management planning techniques to provide a pathway to a predetermined outcome. The military experience illustrates that the ability to control organizational context through rationalized planning is impossible. The British military has recognized the problem and developed an approach that is based on empowering staff situated at the edges of the organization that understand the wider objectives and are empowered to act in accordance with the real-time emerging context without the need to refer back to management for centralized decisions making. This empowering process is encapsulated in the Mission Command methodology. The empowerment of frontline staff creates an agile organization that can feel its way through an emerging context while retaining a focus on effective outcomes. The engagement of the whole organization through Mission Command is held in balance by centralized analysis and control mechanisms that define effects, provide direction, and give clarity of context for individuals to make effective decisions. This approach is practised extensively in comprehensive pre-deployment training that all units go through before being sent on operations.

Being better than the competition

The British military has evolved a methodology that provides competitive advantage through developing cognitive analytical and decision-making processes that allow the organization to act more quickly relative to the competition. These methodologies and processes are shared across North Atlantic Treaty Organization (NATO) forces and provide the framework for multinational co-operation. Marketing literature turns this approach to prime mover advantage where an organization takes advantage of a situation by being the first to act. The British military has embraced this thinking and has evolved structures and processes that support an empowered approach in order to provide competitive advantage. Competitive advantage is gained not through grand strategy but through a number of smaller incremental decisions that eventually gain traction and deliver an overwhelming advantage. Recent operational experiences have witnessed interagency forces access technology that enables an N form organizational approach, thereby providing an asymmetric capability. Where the utilization of technology was a source of competitive advantage for military forces it now needs to be adapted and integrated into social systems that empower more devolved decision making in order to speed the local competitive advantage, therefore Mission Command is even more critical for combating new insurgent capabilities.

Embracing the N form organization allows greater operational agility. In its original World War II incarnation it allowed the maximum utilization of resources. However, with a wider approach it also enables the organization to source and utilize resources and capabilities that otherwise would be beyond the organization's reach. The current and future operational context demands that effective outcomes will require multi-organizational co-operation. The capabilities that are required for state building are a wide spectrum of public and private sector organizations with the military acting as a framework from which the combined effect can be evolved. Although the military may not be the lead organization within this comprehensive framework they will undoubtedly provide essential capability and may well act as the lead change agent within the operational context and therefore it is critical that military leaders understand the wider approach.

The N form requires robust and effective communications to cope with the rapidly evolving situation. Passing new information swiftly across the organization, sharing insight and knowledge to create rapid situational awareness informs better decision making. The passage of information creates insight and informs innovative solutions to complex problems. The combination of individual action and robust communication provides a robust adaptive learning organization; this is essential if an organization such as the British Army is to remain competitive in this demanding environment. The problems of sharing information and creating situational awareness and therefore contextual understanding become more problematic when the organizational force becomes more diverse such as multinational operations. The language, culture, and values that individual organizations apply to interpretation and therefore decision making becomes critical in maintaining shared understanding. The drive for international integration (through NATO, the European Union (EU), and joint training courses) gives recognition to this problem.

Embracing the uncomfortable N form

The military experience of N form organizational transformation (battle grouping) has provided an effective and efficient response to resource limitations. The military has continued to evolve the N form, driving flexibility and adaptation to its lowest level of command. The adoption and adaptation of the N form can be seen clearly in recent operations with the development of hybrid units (units that have a mix of capabilities such as light, airmobile, and heavy brigades focused on a particular task) and this flexible operational response has placed greater demands on equipment and logistic support but has provided the commander with greater flexibility when responding to a volatile environment. The greater the adaptation of the organizational form around the task the better the inter-unit communications and command understanding must be. Operational unity requires a common understanding and shared management practices in order to deploy mixed capabilities effectively at the point of delivery. In short, everyone needs to know how the others will work even if they have never met. The military has to manage the tension between the organizational M form that most of the military utilizes during its steady state, and the N form that is adopted during operations as the standard deployment methodology. This friction can often be identified in the decompression process (when units come back from operations and are reintegrated into the rest of the standard army) where individuals can struggle to reconcile the comparatively limited decision discretion that is offered within an M form organization.

The benefits of examining the transference of key practices from the military to the business space

The demands of the evolving world economy are developing new organizational forms and the N form has many attractions for providing efficiency and new approaches for innovation. Technological advances have provided the opportunity for the N form to become wider and more integrated than previously imagined. The British military has already addressed many of the challenges, ambiguities, and uncertainties; demanding operational environments have forced the military to think beyond the confines of the organic capability of their own organization. The use of technology has evolved new threats (such as al Qaeda's ability to self-organize, co-ordinate attacks, recruit, and raise funding) and offered new opportunities (information gathering, influencing, and detection) that have implications for successful outcomes of military and political action.

The ambiguity of the military context drove the military to think laterally and embrace empowerment and the demands of resource limitations forced them to think differently about organizational design: combined, they merged leadership, command, and management. As previously mentioned, the tension between a resource configuration of task organization (N form) supported by a leadership and management process that maximizes the flexibility opportunities of the organizational response is affected by the natural demands of the central management executives' desire to control. This phenomenon can be identified within the historical developments of techno-logical impact on the battlefield. From the invention of wireless communications through to the evolution of network enabled systems the desire for senior commanders to take control of tactical situations versus the practicalities of information over-load and situational awareness has continuously challenged the benefits of true empowerment of subordinates. The accessibil-ity of network N form capability systems (such as social media) has driven the M form to retain low-level decision loops that speed up the corporate body's decision-making capability (the observe, orient, decide, and act (OODA) loop phenomena) this continuously checks the desire for centralized command and control to overwhelm the empowerment methodology of mis-sion command. This can be adapted to meet the challenges and to understand the limitations of adopting this approach in other organizational contexts.

The demands of N form leadership

N form leadership requires leaders who are prepared to act and make effective decisions in ambiguous and complex situations where information is incomplete and emerging in context. As information became more easily accessible and prevalent, the danger of information overload and decision myopia becomes a problematic issue. Leaders need to be capable of making effective decisions in difficult contexts. The blurring of the organizational structure has meant that leadership needs to be less rigid and more values-driven creating direction while providing the latitude for localization of implementation. Leaders of N form organizations need to maximize the organizational agility while promoting leadership and decision-making empowerment in order to foster innovation. They also need to be risk takers, rule breakers, and lateral thinkers capable of achieving competitive advantage by changing the rules of the game.

Box 2.5   Staff empowerment (Homebase)

When the well-known UK DIY store Homebase became part of the Argos Retail Group in 2002 it introduced a strategy for differentiation through enhanced customer service. (Although Homebase had a reputation for customer service the Argos strategy was to enhance this proposition through top and middle management selection and practices.) They first articulated strong organizational values which included, "putting the customer first, success through teamwork, we make it easy" and importantly "I make a difference." Placing the individual's actions within a strong team culture was important in creating a service delivery philosophy that included:

- The customer is our number 1 priority.
- Look after our customers and they will look after us.
- Everything we do must benefit the customer.
- Treat customers as you would expect to be treated.
- Listen to our customers and go the extra mile.
- We never want our customers to have a wasted journey.

The Homebase strategy was supported and promoted by a number of organizational incentives such as recognition awards, certificates, limited edition pin badges, and vouchers. These promoted the desired behavior and illustrated how the values could be implemented through practical action. The customer service proposition requires continuous renewal in order to obtain and sustain a competitive advantage; this has involved introducing continuous feedback quality loops (very similar to the military's OODA loops). Central to the Homebase strategy is a strong culture of empowerment of frontline staff. Staff members are organized into small local teams that meet and discuss localized issues and these "huddles" are empowered to make decisions and introduce localized service enhancements that are designed to fulfill the organization's value proposition. The team mantra is "I make a difference" and are encouraged to, "take personal responsibility, have a can do attitude, if it's not right – do something about it, own every situation and deal with it, give praise and recognition to everyone's contribution." The emphasis is placed firmly on the individual within a co-ordinated team response and the organizational values are clear, focused, and unambiguous. The Homebase board recognized that centralized decision making would be too slow to delivered the customer experience and accepted that the difference between success and failure would lie with the individual interactions that take place at the local store. They decided to promote empowerment and decentralized decision making in order to achieve their strategy.

Box 2.6   Customer service as a source of differentiation (MFI)

Similarly, MFI, the furniture store, decided to empower local staff to make decisions in order to resolve problems quickly and enhance the customer's experience. In store, staff members are encouraged to resolve complaints from apologizing through to replacements and cash compensation. MFI has been at the forefront of setting and adopting quality industry standards and has encouraged the strap-line "MFI encourages complaint." By understanding complaints local stores, and the company as a whole, can understand what is going on (products, services, consumer behavior) and react appropriately to the evolving situation. The key to MFI's proposition is that no customer should have a poor purchase or service experience when they shop with the company.

As the power of technology introduces severe pressure on pricing strategies many companies are attempting to differentiate their brands through enhanced customer services. As this and the previous example illustrates, this can take place through a range of business activities but what is critical is the shared understanding of the company's values and how these are supported by staff action. Individuals need to then be given discretionary power in order to fulfill these objectives within a range of diverse situations, giving the individual the responsibility to analyze and decide on the best course of action.

Box 2.7 Procter & Gamble's all embracing philosophy

One of the most successful companies in the world is Procter & Gamble (P&G), with a 175-year history of growth. In the past 30 years, P&G has increased its annual sales from US$10 billion to US$82 billion, doubled its number of employees and increased in share price from US$2.32 to US$63. The Chairman of the Board, President and Chief Executive Officer Bob McDonald is a passionate believer in values-based leadership; he has made a number of keynote presentations on this subject and ascribes much to his early years at the United States Military Academy at West Point. Bob McDonald has distilled the P&G values-based leadership model in ten simple steps that drive his leadership activities. These are:

- Living a life driven by purpose is more meaningful and rewarding than meandering through life without direction.
- Everyone wants to succeed, and success is contagious.
- Putting people in the right jobs is one of the most important jobs of the leader.
- Character is the most important trait of a leader.
- Diverse groups of people are more innovative than homogeneous groups.

- Ineffective strategies, systems, and culture are bigger barriers to achievement than the talents of people.
- There will be some people in the organization that will not make it on the journey.
- Organizations must renew themselves.
- Recruiting is the top priority.
- The true test of a leader is the performance of the organization when he or she is absent or after he or she departs.

Bob McDonald's values-based leadership model has been incredibly successful, and the foundations of this approach can clearly be seen in his military experience. The ten key points for leadership have a strong values theme that drives action in the workplace and has been a proven model for delivering sustainable competitive advantage.

Summary

The historical timeline (Figure 2.1) illustrates key events and innovation that enabled transformational knowledge exchange that had a significant impact on social structures. The established organizations that concentrated power through resource control were challenged and radically reconfigured. These transformations modified the relationship between the state, citizen, and the corporation. The industrialization of society enabled non-state aligned interests to become a significant influence and eventually through the globalization of commerce transcend the influence of individual states. This process of liberalization of information and knowledge has changed the dynamics of the state and corporate leadership mindset.

Society had been closely identified with a geographically defined area that shares values, beliefs, and common interests. Leaders needed to reflect the common interest and address the basic needs of the people. However, with the rise of the corporate body the requirements of the corporate leader are substantially different. The increasing desire for maximized profits and shareholder returns has driven leaders to invest their effort in a narrower measure of success.

The growth of organizations that are predominantly concerned with capital has produced the specialist leader (business manager). The growth of capitalism and transactional relationships were solidified within the dominant organizational design (the M form) as this was the most effective model for scientific management practices.

Through resource constraints and the intensity of World War conflict the Germans had to rethink the basic M form structure. They evolved the foundation thinking of the N form by specifying organizational structures and leadership requirements aligned with the task. This transient organizational state had wider implications for leadership, management, operating procedures, culture, and so forth.

After World War II this organizational design drew little attention until NATO faced similar constraints during the height of the Cold War – this began the re-examination of N form military structure which was adopted and enshrined within the process of task organization. This methodology was also supported through the adoption of the German command philosophy of Mission Command, allowing specialists that had been battle grouped together to contribute to the plan and execute independently, if necessary, key aspects of the overall aim of the operation.

The military recognized the organizational agility that N form thinking provided to the modern battlefield. However, it was the advent of social media technology that enabled this thinking to move beyond the confines of the established organizational form. The function of the N form has now evolved beyond physical resources and embraced knowledge sharing through new methods of communications.

This new wave of sharing knowledge has much wider implications for leadership and management (whose thinking is grounded in the old M form) – just as the military has struggled with asymmetric threats from insurgents that can self-organize and share knowledge between non-connected individuals so too are governments and global organizations beginning to have to face the new challenge of the socially connected knowledge exchange economy. (It is important to note that the military embraced

N form organizational design for operational configuration but retained the M form organizational structure.)

Recent civil unrest has been inspired by many issues but the ability to organize, sustain, and co-ordinate action has been facilitated by new social technology. Many a state's reaction has been woefully inadequate (for example, US – Wikileaks, UK – student demonstrations, Spain and Greece – austerity protests, the Arab Spring).

In short, the emerging world needs leaders who base their vision and actions on a coherent values foundation set that resonates across boundaries. The challenges of multicultural corporate organizations pose the question as to the limitations of values-based leadership and the sustainability of management through transaction alone. The dominant Western economies have promoted localized values and specialized agendas that have been adopted as a global standard of shared values. This has formed the basis of internationally accepted approaches in a range of areas from human rights through to trade and environmental protocols. While few would argue as to the value of these standards it can be questioned whose beliefs and interests these standards have been predicated upon.

The historical evolution of social structures informs us as to the significance of transformational change that resonates beyond the significance of localized effect. When new methods of knowledge exchange have emerged radical change has taken place, not only has society accessed new technology that has enabled another wave of change but the world economy witnessed the emergence of new super economic powers that hold different cultures, values, and defined agendas. The importance of values as a basis for informing action must be recognized in order to be effectively managed – differences need to be recognized and a looser affiliation of self-interest must be embraced in order to sustain mutual co-operation.

The military has experienced the challenges of multi-values environments where an imposition of social standards (such as democracy) has proved to be problematic, if the ideals are not grounded on indigenously owned social values the success and longevity of the protocols and ultimately the success of the intervention will become questionable. This has caused the military to re-examine their approach, promoting a more organic self-determination utilizing soft power and transformational leadership in order to encourage the establishment of a functional and stable society.

The military are managing friction between the M form (military, state, third sector, and private sector) organizations and the N form task environment. They recognize the contradictions between the desire for effective management and control and the dangers and rewards of decentralization. New technology and the increased connectivity of the operational environment continue to pose dilemmas for the military leader, perhaps the most valuable insight is how the military select, prepare, and support their leaders to manage the friction. The dynamics of resource control are becoming eclipsed by the enduring battle for hearts and minds, a re-examination of leadership quality that can reach across social and economic divides and facilitate unified action for the greater good must be rediscovered in order to manage the challenges of the global economy.

It is contended that the requirements of the international/global business organization had transcended the military organization form. However, business has reached the limits of a centralized mono-cultural perspective of command and control and paradoxically has begun to re-examine the military experience, the lessons of leadership, and management practices forged in the intensity of conflict in the modern global context. This has provided rich insight into the challenges and opportunities that business can take advantage from. The Western perspective has dominated the global business environment, sharing culture, language, history, and values. New leadership models and methodologies needed to evolve in order to address the looser affiliations of the global framework. As the need for global reach increases, the organizational model and infrastructure need to adapt to take advantage of the global landscape. This has seen an increased level of complexity in recent times with manufacturing, warehousing, research and development, and company headquarters potentially being located in different countries. Through the drive for increased shareholder return and the scrutiny of the global markets companies are taking advantage of the world's resources enabled by the ever-increasing speed of, mainly, communications technology. Although the world has become undoubtedly smaller the key questions of leadership, performance, agility, and efficiency still remain. As the organizational reach and complexity increases the requirement to manage the wider context in a more intuitive and inclusive manner also increases. The international company has a complex internal culture in which it needs to create organizational cohesion, while the leadership requires the skills and methodologies to effectively communicate its intent.

The military's operational experience in this globally connected and complex environment has illustrated key attributes and capabilities that need to be addressed in order to provide effective solutions. The prescriptive, centralized approach cannot map effectively to a true multicultural, multi-values position. The center must provide direction that is ethical, consensual, and legitimate, allowing local individuals to formulate and implement localized action plans. The role of the leader at all levels becomes one of influencing and facilitating, providing clarity and support to individuals to take the initiative within a localized context.

A number of business organizations are embracing a frontline empowered methodology that promotes decentralized decision making as a critical success factor. The British military experience holds valuable lessons for any organization that similarly sees the value in this approach.

Note

1. Christianity is the dominant religious belief in Western civilization. As such it has played a critical role in shaping the values and beliefs of the West. The teachings of Christianity promote caring and sharing, protecting the weak, and leading others for the greater good. It is an inclusive transformational religious perspective. The subservient position of the central figure, Jesus, is a theological perspective that is shared by few other world religions. It can be argued that the birth of the Christian faith is also the beginning of a crystallized articulation of servant leadership in action. The ideas and teaching of Christianity have provided the framework from which societies within the West have evolved their own social structures, ethics, and morality. This in turn has shaped the systems and processes that define our civilization from the modern interpretation of democracy through to international law and universal human rights.

CHAPTER 3

Empowerment and risk as a source of competitive advantage

The N form and task organization methodology builds the foundation for an organization that has agility and is able to respond in a dynamic environment. However, this needs to be supported through empowerment and decentralized decision making in order to take advantage of the opportunity presented in an emerging context.

Technology advances and the evolution of social media have increasingly empowered the individual citizen. Social network platforms enable knowledge exchange, which provides the foundation for N form organization response. Technology has provided the gateway for a new form of social order that will require a greater emphasis on leadership with less focus on traditional command and control. As social networks self-determine commitment and the individual within the network harnesses collective resources, this can be a highly effective form of direct action through collaboration. These network-enabled responses have significant expediential capabilities that can be quickly co-ordinated around an emerging issue.

The concept of defining and articulating effects is a useful concept in gaining cross-boundary support even when individual actors do not share common end states. Diverging agendas can be reconciled through transitional co-operation beyond the facilitation of a state or organizational affiliation. New networks are emerging based on the connectivity and interaction of social discourse. Once the preserve of technologically advanced nations, these capabilities have now gained significant traction in emerging economies and have witnessed a significant adoption by the world's population.

This chapter examines the requirements of empowering individuals and teams to deliver competitive advantage through devolved decision making. For some organizations, building an agile response to rapidly emerging situations can provide an invaluable source of competitive advantage. Developing the themes established in Chapters 1 and 2, this chapter explores the military's approach to developing high-performance teams and the benefits and potential limitations for business. Social networks combined with task organization of resources require devolved decision making as the task within the context is emerging and the opportunity to act is transient. Therefore, decentralization of decision making and resource allocation must be a critical consideration.

The emerging utilization of N form organizational structures is highlighting tensions between the M form's managerial desire for centralized control against the necessity to reach out to the limits of the wider organization in order to shorten the response time in emerging or fleeting opportunities.

How to build a winning business

A prime requirement for a successful business is in finding a basis for a competitive advantage. This can be achieved in a number of ways, new product development, service innovation, identification of new markets, or a lower production cost base. Whatever the source of competitive advantage the pursuit, identification, and effective implementation will be critical in determining continued success. Identifying competitive advantage is a continuous process of renewal and examination; rarely does an organization have sole ownership of a source of competitive advantage. The constant battle for improvement is present in all markets, although the source of the advantage may be very different depending on the nature of the product or service and the nature of the market it serves. Often an organization that prevails in a market as the dominant party has a number of areas across the business where it performs as well as any other and some where it consistently performs better than its main competitors. So, for many the source of competitive advantage is not the preserve of a single factor but is spread over many areas of the business. For example, the Resource-Based View (RBV) approach to strategy highlights that one way of achieving a competitive advantage is for it to be based on the way an organization performs its internal processes, practices, and behaviors. It is argued that such factors are more difficult for a competitor to identify and hence replicate.

The key is to optimize as many aspects of the organization's performance relative to the competition. The concept of competitive relativity is critical in building a sustainable competitive advantage and is at the heart of the military methodology.

Getting everyone involved

Unlocking new ways of engaging the organization in the pursuit and attainment of competitive advantage that leads to increasing shareholder value (or demonstrating value for money through efficient and effective service delivery in the public sector) is a key responsibility of management. The old adage "two heads are better than one" reminds us that engaging everyone in the pursuit of competitive advantage is a powerful resource. For an organization to be continuously renewing its position and remaining competitive, a culture of critical evaluation and innovation must be engrained in order to encourage everyone to participate. Leaders must utilize the management process to create focus and develop a culture of inclusion and sense of ownership for individuals to feel their contribution will be recognized and valued. As previously mentioned, the source of competitive advantage can often lie in small margins of performance, resources, or knowledge. It is through the identification, adoption, and promotion of these capabilities (linked to a focused, facilitative leadership methodology) that promotes management to reach beyond the transactional interface and energizes individuals to search for answers.

Getting involved the military way

The British military has evolved methods of engaging the wider organizational capability in order to achieve a sense of ownership and inclusion. Utilizing servant leadership the organization is committed to individual development and self-betterment, individuals are encouraged to get involved and take on new responsibility, to participate in all aspects of the process. This empowers the individual to act, by describing the wider context and the intent of the commanding officer and/or the organization, and individuals are given tasks that are linked to wider outcomes. The process of identifying and describing higher levels of action allows the individual to position their task and activity within a wider framework thus giving greater emphasis and importance to their contribution. No longer does an individual feel he/she is a small cog in a big machine but rather the essential component that makes the whole thing work. Mission Command promotes the importance of the individual's contribution to the wider successful outcomes and gives latitude to the individual to examine the task within the wider context and actively drive the solution. It demands the active involvement of the individual and rejects the passive acceptance of direction. This level of engagement and proactive involvement requires high levels of trust to exist both up and down, through the organization, and between individuals.

Mission Command is an inclusive and expansive methodology that requires strong leadership with nurturing qualities. A sense of achievement in the development of others must be central to the values of the organization for sustainment can only be achieved through continuous renewal and search for advancement. The wider collective or "team first" approach has strong attractions for motivating higher order engagement (motivational theory), however, this must be owned and consistently demonstrated by the leadership function. It must be an inner belief as the temptation of transactional advancement will muddy the approach and demote the concept to a management function and in time erode the validity of the approach.

This highlights the importance of trust; although this subject will be returned to several times during this chapter it is important to recognize that high levels of individual and collective trust must exist and be sustained in order for optimized team performance to be sustained.

Trust: the elephant in the management room

Understanding how to build trust and accept limited risk-taking strategies in order to deliver innovation is a significant management issue. For many individuals in management trust is an uncomfortable concept as a management function – most people like to think they are considered trustworthy. The subject is not widely discussed within professional business development courses but it is of the utmost importance. Trust has multidimensional considerations with, first, the individual; are they trustworthy and do I trust them? This question considers whether the individual portrays the attributes and characteristics that are perceived to be trustworthy, do they behave in a way that demonstrates they can be trusted; this question also begs the question, what is the individual to be trusted with? Already the concept of trust becomes a fluid and personal evaluative construct. Second, does the organization trust them, do they have authority to act, make decisions, and are they empowered to exercise power on behalf of the organization? This is most overtly demonstrated in positional titles as these convey the parameters of preconceived trust demonstrated through authority. Third, are the behaviors of the individual congruent with the authority paradigm of the organizational context? Do they behave in a way that is compatible with the level of trust place upon them by the organization? They should not only conduct managerial tasks in line with the prescriptive operational policies of the company but must also act in keeping with the ethical and values framework that would be expected of the individual occupying that position. The fourth aspect of trust is experience. If individuals have had a poor experience of trust they will be reluctant to commit their trust again. Fifth, and perhaps most significantly, is the organization's trustworthiness. Has the organization acted in keeping with its own policies, practises, and procedures? Has it acted in a consistent and transparent way that validates the trust that individuals place in the corporate? Trust is a learned validated engagement – it can be very fragile if not actively managed.

Box 3.1   Trust

A colleague of mine once had a very poor experience working with a newly-appointed director within a professional-services company. He had worked for many years for the business and was a highly-committed employee, he believed in placing the interests of the company and subordinates in front of his own personal interests. His view had always been that if you act in the best interest of the organization you work for then you will contribute positively to the organization's success. During the time he worked with this director he witnessed behavior and decisions that were not in the interest of the business. The director often manipulated situations, management figures, or verbal exchanges in order to benefit his own agenda. This form of toxic leadership[1] quickly eroded trust and my colleague felt unable to support the individual with conviction because he knew the director acted illegitimately for the level of authority that had been invested in him. The deterioration of trust was compounded when senior members of the organization learnt about the director's behavior. Despite this knowledge the organization did not act or sanction the director's behavior. The failure to act on behalf of the senior leaders eroded faith and trust in the whole organization, this process deconstructed commitment and undermined innovation.

The selection of leaders who have strong values and beliefs that are shared by the collective and perceived as legitimate builds high levels of trust through consistent action and decision making. The faith placed on team performance reinforces the need for the leader to act in the wider interest in order for success to be achieved.

These traits become ingrained in the organization's culture and become organizational values that are upheld and promoted through reward and recognition. It is from these foundations that the military project leadership and management methods that allow the fluid response to emerging situations in complex contexts. The flexible and agile response of the military deployed on operations is based on a maneuverist approach that captures an attitude to conflict of efficiency; pitting your strengths against your opponent's weaknesses.

The adoption of maneuverist thinking and the wider implications

For hundreds of years the British military has enjoyed an enviable track record of achieving success in the most challenging environments. Much of the British military's success has been due to individual actions or inspired resilience of groups of individuals bound together through a strong culture. It would be a fair observation that individual discretion has not always been the accepted practise within the military. However, the adoption of maneuverist[2] thinking adopted in the 1980s during the end of the Cold War period, and inspired by the efficiency and operational performance of the German Army in the latter stages of World War II, has driven a more decentralized, intuitive response. Accepting that the maintenance of a large standing modern military force was rapidly becoming unsustainable the West began to re-examine how previous military forces had managed the dilemma and this triggered the resurgence of German military thinking.

The cornerstone to the adoption of the German methodology was the unmatchable size of the former Soviet Union military force during the Cold War (1946–1991). Although the Soviet Union had comparatively less sophisticated equipment they used a simple grand strategic plan that focused on deep strike[3] and grand strategic maneuver warfare similar to the Soviet offensive of 1944. The Germans had responded with localized maneuvers of combined battle groups, which was highly effective but lacked depth and suffered from their higher command's imposed restrictions on "holding ground" nullifying their ability to utilize maneuver warfare effectively to counter the Soviet strike. The tables had turned. The Germans had been the architects of the *blitzkrieg* (lightning war) utilizing combined capabilities and rapid advances during the staggering military success they enjoyed in the early part of the war and yet it was the Soviet army that mastered the technique at the strategic level.

Looking for answers to today's questions in lessons from the past

Considering the Germans were defeated in World War II and suffered a resounding defeat on the Eastern front it may be surprising that the NATO Forces adopted the German military command philosophy. A number of factors drew the commanders to their conclusion. First, the West could trade space for tactical advantage (the Germans were told to hold ground) and the

West had better balanced maneuver forces and inter-operability between units. This allowed military units to respond, regroup and provide localized superior concentrated capability. The analysis concluded that the Soviet Union needed to achieve strategic success quickly because of its limited logistic and equipment capability and, therefore, the West needed to blunt and slow the advance sufficiently to allow the weaknesses inherent within the Soviet forces to cause stagnation. The West could then use their greater technical sophistication to deliver point strikes that would render the larger military land forces irrelevant. A very good example of the maneuverist concept in action against a numerically larger force was the first Iraq war of 1991.

The first and last Cold War

It has been said that the 1991 Iraq war was the last war of the Cold War and heralded the beginning of post-Cold War modern conflict. The greater utilization of technology to rapidly gather and assimilate information was first thought to indicate a more centralized command and control paradigm. However, the reverse was true. In ensuing conflicts such as Croatia (1991–1995), Bosnia (1992–1995), Iraq (2003–) and Afghanistan (2001–), technology became a double-edged sword. Not only did it provide the platform for maneuver forces to rapidly exchange information and concentrate force effectively, it also provided the capability for much smaller forces to take evasive action and provide a non-conventional response. This thinking led to the current situation where conventional troops, insurgency, terrorism, and irregular militia all blurred to provide a highly complex non-linear operating environment. This unconventional spectrum of combat became aligned with a non-traditional operating methodology known as asymmetric warfare. As the name suggest, asymmetric warfare is non-equal, where one side seeks to pursue their military and political aims by exploiting an adversary's weaknesses or differences such as size, logistics, or political mandate. The 9/11 terrorist attacks on the World Trade Center are an example of a terrorist group pursuing individual political aims through non-conventional means. The attacks provided a greater impact than any conventional military response with such limited capability.

Out with the old and in with the new

The experience of the Iraq war convinced modern armies that high-tech precision weapons combined with high levels of co-ordination and inter-operable platforms provided a high impact capability and the best return on investment for limited national defense budgets. The Balkans conflict consisted of a number of smaller conflicts from 1991 to 1995 and was typified by the complex internal struggles of individual factions. The full range of combatant capabilities were present within this volatile conflict and presented a new challenge to military thinking. The Balkans conflict signified the end of traditional large-scale conflict that had typified almost a century of European and Global conflict and heralded a new asymmetrical or, as Rupert Smith (2005) termed it, "War among the people."

The Iraq war facilitated greater technical and methodological integration between Western military forces. However, it was the complexity of the Balkans that facilitated the adaptation and innovation of the conceptual approach. Maneuver thinking needed to be adapted to a localized peace enforcement and state-building effect. The lessons learned would be severely tested in the subsequent Iraq and Afghanistan conflicts.

Conceptually, the military recognized the benefits of technology and also the potential limitations posed by information overload and clouding of timely decision making. As environments became more irregular and operationally more complex the increased reliance on decentralized decision making became fundamental to success. The ability for a single action to have wide-reaching strategic consequences has been facilitated by the rapid development and expansion of mass media. The experiences of these conflicts played out in front of mass international audiences gave birth to the concept of "the strategic corporal" as never before had the individual actions of relatively low-level commanders carried such significance to the overall success of the military campaign.

How strategy was changed from a prison

The events that took place at the Iraq Abu Ghraib prison in 2004 shocked the world. Seymour Hersh published an article in the New Yorker Magazine that reported abuse including sexual abuse, torture, and sodomy. These allegations were supported by photographic evidence that had been taken by the abusers themselves. The shocking revelation instantly became front-page news around the world. The reports caused concern and consternation in many parts of the world but had the most significant impact on Arab nations. Those nations that had serious concerns over the legitimacy of the initial invasion now felt vindicated, as the liberators became the persecutors, replacing one oppressive regime with another. Undoubtedly, the events at the Abu Ghraib prison influenced domestic attitudes to the conflict and provided tacit support for the insurgent-led conflict that engulfed Iraq during this period. Millions of people became informed of the events that had taken place in a single prison and carried out by approximately 10 to 16 individuals. These reports had a significant strategic impact on the conduct of the campaign and the perception of legitimacy of the military intervention. Abu Ghraib and other events that took place during the military operation reinforced the view that individuals operating on the front line could have a huge strategic impact. Technology has enabled the capture and broadcast of events in real time. This instantaneous news generation capability made a high proportion of the world's population aware of these events and profoundly influenced public opinion. It was the same technology that provided the foundation for self-determined insurgency capability to have significant international military and political impact.

Embracing the danger

The requirements for commanders to trust and empower subordinates took on new significance. Recognizing that it would be impossible to train all soldiers for all situations the importance of individual decision making became more important. The term "doing the right thing" has become a common phrase that indicates the values foundation framework from which individuals are expected to draw their guidance when making decisions in complex and volatile environments. The greater emphasis on values as a guiding principle for decision making was signaled by the introduction of a process of teaching values and standards within the British Army. This formal articulation provided clarity and a shared understanding of what was to be expected. These shared values are largely shared across all members of NATO and provide a unified view of how military campaigns should be conducted.

Innovation often involves risk and managing risk requires individuals to understand how to identify, mitigate, and accept risk. The business practitioner who can accept and control risk will be better prepared to exploit the complexity and uncertainty of the modern business landscape. The creative process involves individuals offering their innermost thoughts, experiences, and suggestions and this level of intimate exposure is often inhibited if high levels of trust do not exist. The process of creative innovation has risk of exposure to potential ridicule or disappointment if the individual is not assured of respect for his/her views.

The cornerstone to success

The British military has evolved a complex and sophisticated approach to achieving success; this is based on experience and reflective practise, however, the key principles can be crystallized in three key themes.

First, the British military select their officers at a comparatively young age with a strong emphasis on values-based leadership. The individual needs to demonstrate a genuine concern for others along with the ability to facilitate change and lead others in the pursuit of the greater good. The organization then trains the individual to be an effective manager; this approach gives a strong emphasis on leadership instead of on transactional management.

Second, by selecting leaders using a comprehensive and enduring methodology the organization has evolved a culture that promotes, recognizes, and rewards behaviors that are aligned with these values. Over time the British military has evolved a strong and coherent culture that clearly reflects the values and standards of the organization. Combining leadership selection and organizational culture with shared values, individuals quickly build trust that is supported and sustained through consistent behavior and transparent decision making.

Third, the values-based leadership and the comprehensive culture allow the organization to deploy implementation methodologies and management practises that utilize the benefits of a high-trust relationship. Trust enables the organization to empower frontline staff to make decisions as the emerging situation demands, ensuring that decision loops are kept short and the organization remains agile and responsive to fleeting opportunities. It is the combination of leadership, culture, and appropriate methodologies that gives the British military a competitive advantage in complex and volatile environments.

Identification of risk and the appropriate management of risk for innovation

The concept of risk is an individual, group, and organizational cultural construct. The individual has perceptions of risk based on a number of factors including experience, previous outcomes, and training. The group will perceive risk dependent on the time the group has been together, shared experience, and the homogeneity of the group's values, aims, and objectives. The organization's perspective regarding risk will largely be based on external factors such as markets, the threat and cost of litigation, impact of mistakes on the business, and the level of competition. Risk is a multidimensional construct, however, innovation and top-level team performance requires risk to be accepted in order to achieve competitive advantage. Management of risk has a direct association with levels of trust; the higher levels of trust the more effectively risk can be managed.

As previously mentioned, the engagement of the entire organization's intellectual and physical resources in the pursuit of the organization's aims is an imperative in today's current operational environment. The process of empowerment is more than a diffusion of power or decision making; empowerment involves the individual's commitment to contribute. Empowerment accepts risk by both the organization and the individual; it is implemented through leadership and validated through management action.

The British military has evolved a decentralized decision-making process that flattens the organizational structure making the corporate body more adaptive and agile. The military has recognized that technology has provided a disruptive platform that enables small groups of individuals to organize the production of sophisticated responses. This has driven the need for greater empowerment, individuals need to act independently and share information effectively across the organization. The responsibility for observing, understanding, and synthesizing this information into meaningful communications that informs the understanding of the wider context becomes the responsibility of the individual. The availability of communications and complex knowledge resources has engaged a larger number of actors in this knowledge generation and active sharing process than ever before. Frontline soldiers are now expected to understand the gravitas of events as they unfold, they need to be active in the reporting system and be prepared to act without instruction in order to achieve the overall aims of the organization.

Keeping decision-making where it counts

Through engaging all members of the organization the knowledge generation capability is dramatically improved. It is important to remember that the universally connected organization needs to remain agile through management that is inclusive and generates a small number of rapid decision loops that ensure empowerment and that decision making is kept to the frontline of the organization. The military has utilized a process known as the OODA loop to generate meaningful actions within context. The theory of OODA loops was first described by a US Air Force pilot, John Boyd, who observed the OODA phenomena in the contest between MIG and F-86 pilots; simply put, the F-86 aircraft had better observation capabilities and generated better combat superiority. The pilot was able to observe, orientate, decide and act more quickly than his opponent, therefore creating a sustainable competitive combat advantage. (The OODA loop is discussed in greater detail in Chapter 5.) The key is the utilization of a methodology that is placed at the heart of the decision-making process ensuring that decisions are made on better information and made more quickly relative to your opponent. Decisions based on emerging information that are implemented more quickly and more efficiently will eventually overwhelm the opposition's ability to make meaningful decisions.

This kind of capability has a wide application within the commercial world and would offer a number of key advantages to a business that adopts such techniques. The OODA loop means that the gap between an organization's service delivery and client interface can be shortened thus providing real-time feedback to main boards. This methodology allows for a better understanding of the dynamics of the markets and the changing patterns of consumer behavior. Effective sharing of insight gained through shared situational awareness can inform other critical functions of the business such as logistics, research and development, and customer service strategy. Empowering the decision-making process enables specialist areas to utilize resources more effectively in order to produce an appropriate response. The mixture of empowerment, decision making, and knowledge sharing is not an intuitive trait but a process that needs to be taught and learned and then sustained through management practise and cultural adoption.

The full utility of empowered decision making can only be fully realized if the organization has management and organizational structures that support the process. Resources must be allocated through a flexible priority system, reserves must be maintained and only committed when the emerging market situation dictates that a competitive advantage can be achieved and a suitable return on the assets will be obtained. The process of communication becomes even more important to an organization that wishes to adopt this agile approach. For communication to be effective it is a *sine qua non* that a variety of approaches that reflect the needs of different audiences must be used. To this end it becomes critical that the message(s) are delivered using appropriate language (i.e., has meaning to the recipient such that they know what is expected of them and why) and that the frequency (i.e., timeliness) of the message is appropriate. It is important to remember that the communication protocols must act in all directions (downwards, upwards, and across) within the organization and where necessary recognize the appropriate communication channels between organizations. The growing use of management terminology and corporate abbreviations does not help the process of clear communications and should be discouraged. It would be a justifiable observation to point to the development of the MBA as a significant step towards meeting some of these challenges. However, the diversity of approaches and taught methodologies from business school to business school has negated some of these benefits and in some cases has exacerbated the issue.

Acting on what is important

As mentioned previously gaining operational information effectively helps to provide strategic insight that, in turn, can deliver the focus to obtain a critical decision point. It is important that frontline staff utilize a structured approach and recognized channels for communication, ensuring that important information is "fast tracked" up the organization to key decision makers. This process can be enhanced through the development of indicators of critical information that individuals understand are essential to the attainment of the organization's plan. The development of critical information of market indicators is a helpful method of highlighting key activities or events that could happen at any time. They help to illustrate to the individual what is important. Stating that the change in consumer behavior is important does not have as much meaning as "tell me as soon as people start to swap from product A to product B" – even more helpful if they can tell you why they swap.

Sharing information across the organization builds corporate knowledge, shared situational awareness, and capitalizes on success. In order for cross-communication to be effective it must be structured, concise, and have clarity of meaning and purpose. It is important for the recipient to understand how this information is of use to them for the individual to implement the content effectively.

Remember, without trust, individuals will only tell you what they think you want to hear, you must create an environment of dialog and ensure individual's feedback, observation, and assessment is valued and acted on. Leadership should ensure credit and positive feedback is constantly given to ensure best practice is maintained.

As a consultant I (Ivan) worked closely with a large corporate communications team. Although the team had many tasks to perform essentially they were responsible for communicating information about the business to the markets and also communicating information from the corporate center out to all members of the business. After working on a number of programs with this team it became clear that the organization had developed a number of differentiated and conflicting communications channels. These included staff magazines, bulletins, press releases, and e-mails. Different company locations had also developed localized communications channels such as a "the Friday meeting" or staff office boards to supplement the official channels. The communications team struggled with delivering timely information in the right format effectively. This in turn led to mixed messages being passed out to the markets via staff communications and working practises. This organic growth of corporate communications channels is mirrored in many businesses but the evolution of "broadcast channels" has forced many organizations to rethink their communications protocols. Unfortunately, much of this thinking has been directed around control (such as the use of group e-mails) and not enough time has been spent on structure and content in order to deliver effective communications.

Box 3.2　How little ideas can become big ones!

Competitive advantage often exists at the margins of business operations. Although some products and services can be well established, innovation can be the source of future business success. This point was well made in 1950 by Richard P. Carlton, Former CEO, 3M Corporation, when he said, "Our company has, indeed, stumbled onto some of its new products. But never forget that you can only stumble if you're moving."

3M is quite possibly the most innovative company of our times that even CEOs of other visionary companies admire. 3M initially failed in its mining business, and eventually stumbled onto most of the successful innovations that we know 3M for, including Post-It Notes, masking tape, and Scotch tape. According to Collins and Porras (1994), "Although the invention of the Post-it Note might have been somewhat accidental, the creation of the 3M environment that allowed it was anything but an accident."

3M institutionalized such mechanisms to drive innovation as: the "15 per cent rule" – technical people spend up to 15 per cent of their time on projects of their own choosing or initiative; the "25 per cent rule" – each division should produce 25 per cent of annual sales from new products and services introduced in the previous five years (which later increased to 30 per cent); and the "Golden Step" award – given to those creating successful new business ventures originated within 3M. More growth mechanisms were created to stimulate internal entrepreneurship, test new ideas, create unplanned experimentation, share new ideas, develop new innovation, cross-fertilize technology, ideas and innovation, stimulate innovation via customer problems, speed product development and market introduction cycles, provide profit sharing, and promote "a small company within a big company feel" by creating small autonomous business units and product divisions – over a dozen business processes to stimulate creativity, innovation and growth – in early 1990 3M had over 60,000 products and over 40 separate product divisions.

A key point in this example is that it is only through the existence of trust that a company such as 3M can be innovative and accept risk taking as part of the culture. In order to achieve this management structures, processes, reward systems, leadership, and value sets need to be aligned to deliver the desired behaviors. This results in an organization where individuals feel that they can trust their leadership and the very organization itself and, as such, are prepared to accept and take risks through innovation. Equally, the leadership knows that they can trust staff not to abuse the levels of trust that are invested in them.

Consequently, this becomes a virtuous circle that is built upon trust and empowerment at all levels throughout the organization.

Importance of empowerment and responsibility acceptance

The organization's leadership must promote empowerment of the individual. However, this is more than the diffusion of power, it is the delegation of responsibility and the giving of clear direction (objective setting). How and in what ways individuals are empowered will depend on the type of organization, its culture, its markets (requirement and benefits), and personal relationships. The development of this infrastructure and organizational capability is a key management function. Like communications, empowerment needs a methodology in which it can be effectively facilitated and understood. The development of standardized planning and decision-making tools helps the process of transparency and increases confidence and commitments of the wider community.

The British military uses a combination of processes in order to facilitate a comprehensive and agile response. The adoption of the conceptual framework of "the comprehensive approach" expands the context to fully appreciate the wider implications of the problem. The application of appropriate planning tools allows for complex tasks and operations to be planned and managed within this context. The development of a strong team ethic embedded within a culture of trust and risk acceptance enables the utilization of an empowered implementation methodology termed Mission Command. This simple process and organizational traits combine to develop approaches that accept change, focus on the development of overall effects, and allow for operational objectives to be modified thus providing the optimum solution based on the emerging context.

Although planning methodology and Mission Command will be expanded in Chapter 5 it is important to understand the concept of effects as opposed to task-based planning.

How effects can achieve better objectives

Effects-based planning defines an "end state" rather than a route map of how to achieve specific objectives. This enables the individual to exercise discretion and actively participate in the decision-making process. It is important to recognize that effects-based planning requires a shared understanding of terminology, defining an effect such as "secure" or "defend" must be understood by the recipient.

As an example, imagine a situation where two cars had collided, a number of people were injured, a forest fire had broken out, a Scout group had a nearby summer camp, and a number of holiday homes were located in the area. This hypothetical scenario presents a number of complex problems. Initial analysis may establish a number of priorities and an allocation of resources to tasks, such as call the ambulance services to deal with the car accident, the fire brigade to put out the fire, and the police to inform the residents and the scouts. However, if the problem is compounded by the addition of wider events or a restriction of resources the situation may need to be dealt with in a very different way.

Imagine being the strategic commander, dealing with a hundred such tasks then, instead of listing priorities and resource allocations you could well utilize an effects-based approach. This could entail directing a local officer to "secure the area" where "secure the area" allows for greater discretion. The local commander may well use local knowledge to set priorities and direct events in a different pattern in order to achieve the desired effect. This may involve synchronization of assets or acceptance of risk based on experience, training, and context. The localized commander understands the commander's intent through the interpretation of the effect, they then conduct a localized analysis and make a decision, and this provides the framework of a plan that is then implemented through a Mission Command methodology.

The localized commander may well direct the fire brigade and ambulance to deal with the car accident and task a local inhabitant to inform the Scouts and the local residents to self-evacuate, this may involve utilizing the Scouts' organizational structure to co-ordinate the evacuation. Local knowledge may have identified a natural firebreak in the forest such as a river and therefore negate the requirement to fight the fire. The approach accepts risk but provides a better utilization of scarce resources in order to meet the higher commander's intent.

The utilization of effects-based planning provides clear guidance of the higher commander's intention without the requirement of detailed planning and resource allocation. The articulation of intent through the description of an effect speeds up the planning cycle by empowering the subordinate commanders to conduct their own analysis and plan within a framework. The local commander has better local situational awareness and is better prepared to develop plans that are appropriate and identify risk and building in redundancy where needed.

Empowerment actively accepts risk as part of the organizational culture. Risk is shared by both the organization and the individual and requires an understanding of this interconnectivity. In order to empower individuals effectively, an understanding of risk must exist. Risk is a relative concept and an individual's ability to cope with risk depends on a number of variables including training, previous exposure, previous outcomes, and an understanding of the operational context. Empowerment requires individuals to actively accept responsibility; they must understand the risk they are taking on behalf of the organization and be prepared to justify their decisions within the wider context of mutual organizational benefits. A breakdown in trust can have far reaching consequences and this is not confined to the military.

Trust and empowerment but is it all about the money?

Nick Leeson was a derivatives trader for the UK's oldest bank, Barings. He used the bank's funds to make increasingly risky speculative trades. At first his trades paid off, the huge dividends initially made the bank over £10 million accounting for over 10 per cent of the bank's yearly income. At the time, Leeson's salary was £50,000 and he enjoyed a £130,000 bonus for his efforts that year. His speculative professional practise soon turned sour and in an attempt to rectify his mistakes he became increasingly desperate and engaged in more and more high-risk trades that dramatically increased Baring's liability. In 1995 the full extent of Leeson's behavior became apparent, Leeson's activities shocked the banking world when Barings collapsed announcing losses of £827 million.

Leeson's behavior demonstrated a lack of trust in the organization, his motivation superficially appears to be monetary return but Leeson later confessed that a great deal of his behavior was largely driven by the desire to maintain his status and the esteem he enjoyed within the bank. Leeson felt unable to admit to his mistakes preferring to risk everything in an attempt to rectify the situation. Baring's experience signaled the introduction of greater regulation and supervision of individual traders. However, the recent events in the sub-prime market demonstrate the problems of attempts to modify individual behaviors through self-regulation.

Organizations such as Barings and many other financial institutions had evolved an organizational culture that was over reliant on financial reward as a key motivator. Prestige and status were largely driven by fee income, although this culture cannot be blamed solely for Leeson's actions it undoubtedly contributed significantly not only to his actions but also to the lack of supervision and regulation that others applied at the time.

The nature of the business operation defines the benefits and requirements of risk taking. This needs to be supported with strong organizational cultures that have embedded a wider ethical responsibility; leaders must exercise a fine balance of empowerments and good quality managerial practise.

The case of Nick Leeson illustrates the limitations of transactional management, how it failed to recognize the need for a wider, more inclusive ethical and values perspective and also provides a window as to how people were valued and rewarded at Barings.

Organizational agility for operational efficiency

The nature of the military task requires risk-taking; managing risk-taking can help performance and improve outcomes and is hugely improved through training and experience. The British military has developed a methodical approach to developing individuals' ability to manage risk effectively and appropriately. The British military achieve management of risk through individual and collective training and managed exposure, combined with a shared utilization of analytic tools and shared implementation methodologies. Units are effectively managed through a process of "pre-deployment" training. This is a process that first refreshes and augments the individual's skills and then builds core-team functions. This can involve low-level collective training (eight man section level) supported by specialist skills (such as medical, signals, or driver training) to provide the foundation capability that is required to function effectively within the operational environment. Small teams are then fused together through collective training. Units are built around the operational requirements, utilizing the "battlegroup" organizational structure and are increasingly augmented with non-military specialists that provide transferable skills within a societal construct. At each level the teams are tested through exercises and training that provide the framework for individuals to test skills, build mutual trust, and develop the operational organizational culture that supports team cohesion. Pre-deployment training also revises and tests decision-making and management methodologies in order to ensure that utilization and implementation is as efficient as possible and provides operational competitive advantage.

Central to the British military's approach of decentralized command philosophy (Mission Command) is the understanding that centralized decision-making cannot cope with the complexities of a volatile environment where multiple emerging situations require analysis and decisions to be made in real time. The shorter the decision implementation process the more agile the organizational response to an emerging situation. However, agility alone does not guarantee successful outcomes; it is a combination of quality decentralized leadership (values-based leadership), effective decision-making (such as campaign planning, the seven questions process[4] and rapid implementation (Mission Command)) that outperforms the competition. This kind of decentralized decision-making requires a strong organizational culture in order to provide a foundation within which flexible and adaptive systems can be grounded.

Transferring these key concepts from the military space to the business environment must be sensitively managed, adapted, and measured. The military need empowerment in order to achieve competitive advantage and derive this from the advantage of localized recruitment, strong homogenous culture, and very defined outputs (although the range of outputs for military forces is becoming far wider in current operations). Business recognizes the benefits of empowerment in order to release the benefits of the organizational intellectual capital. However, business is driven by different criteria for measuring success. Although these measurements of success can vary greatly from organization to organization much of modern business management theory and practise has been focused on producing efficiency and mitigating risk. This approach is adequate in a stable and benign environment but in the increasingly volatile global market few organizations can enjoy such an operational context. Success for business is increasingly reliant on innovation and the development of cultures, methodologies, and practises that support and renew innovation.

Notes

1. An individual who abuses the leader–follower relationship and leaves the group in a worse position than when they first assumed the leadership role.
2. The maneuverist approach is defined as an approach to operations in which shattering the enemy's overall cohesion and will to fight is paramount. It calls for an attitude of mind in which doing the unexpected, using initiative, and seeking originality is combined with a ruthless determination to succeed (MoD, 1996).
3. This is a process that co-ordinates military assets to attack targets that are deep behind the frontline, these are often command locations, supply, or logistic centers. Generally they are less well protected but have significant military importance. The successful prosecution of a deep-strike campaign coupled with an aggressive ground offensive can be highly effective as a maneuverist strategy.
4. Both the campaign plan and the seven questions are analytical tools that the military use to help define the problem and to develop a number of possible planning solutions before making a command decision. Both are discussed later in this book in more detail (Chapter 5).

CHAPTER 4

Culture: an essential framework for output performance

When the charismatic US President, John. F. Kennedy said "Ask not what your country can do for you – ask what you can do for your country" in his 1961 inaugural speech he made an impassioned and memorable speech to the nation. His words called for a renewed commitment from the individuals of the nation, to combine in a common purpose, commit to a goal beyond the transactional relationship of management and strive for transformational engagement.

These words reflected the tensions in post-World War II US: the emerging threat of the USSR, the escalation of the Vietnam War, and the internal social and racial tensions of the country. The rallying cry attempted to reverse the perceived disengagement of the American public with the high levels of social cohesion that had defined the previous 50 years. The President recognized that the American culture was changing and this would pose problems for his administration in meeting the emerging challenges.

President Kennedy recognized the importance of a cohesive organizational culture and the benefits it provided in meeting the challenges of an increasingly threatening and competitive environment. The charismatic leader attempted to set the tone and create a vision that the individual could believe in and share, thus creating a renewed nation with strong shared values that would be resilient to these ensuing challenges.

All organizations have a culture; these cultures support and promote individual and collective behaviors that are identified as appropriate, however, little attention is given to this

critical subject in many professional management development training programs. The military has evolved a strong
and distinctive culture and this chapter examines the benefits
and pitfalls of organizational culture and identifies the key
components that combine to shape and actively manage that
culture.

Why consider culture?

Often a single organization will have several sub-cultures that
have evolved over a period of time. Organizational culture is
influenced by a number of factors including dominant leadership traits, function, structure, and process. Culture can be
both a powerful asset and an organizational constraint. The
key issue is aligning culture against the requirements of the
operational context. Friction occurs when an organization has
evolved a culture that is no longer appropriate for the context.
As financial performance is a key business management issue
the sustainability of the organization is closely linked to effective management of the organizational culture. There are many
definitions of culture. Cameron and Quinn offer the following
definition:

> An organizational culture is reflected by what is valued. The
> dominant leadership style, the language and symbols, the
> procedures and routines, and the definitions of success that
> make an organization unique.   (1999, p. 15)

This definition offers a good grounded perspective of the wide-
ranging nature of organizational culture. All aspects of the
business from individuals through to structures and policies
and procedures contribute significantly to how an individual
understands the culture of the organization. The mapping and
classification of culture also provides valuable insight into the
individual and sometimes localized nature of culture.

A key role for business management is understanding corporate
culture and being effective at actively managing that culture in
order to optimize operational performance. Critical to success
is an appropriate organizational culture for the competitive

operating context; aligning culture with the requirements and demands of the wider context is a prime management function. As culture resonates with individuals and promotes commitment beyond the immediate task the establishment and active management of culture should be a strategic decision for business leadership. It is important to recognize that although organizations will reflect a dominant cultural style it is more complex than initial investigation would suggest. Individual teams and sub-organizations will often reflect unique, individual cultures that are at odds with the overarching organizational culture. This non-alignment of cultures and sub-cultures can cause "friction" within the organization and require careful management in order to achieve optimum operational performance.

The British military has evolved simple systems for altering team and organizational culture during operational deployments. This kind of cultural manipulation delivers operational performance while retaining the key sustaining components of the wider organizational culture.

Business leaders need to understand the importance of effectively managing culture. With the rise of international and global organizations the internal sensitivities and complexities of sub-cultures need to be recognized and actively engaged in order to achieve optimized business performance.

Working with culture

The professional management of an organization requires frequent change and implementation of new methods and practices. Change management can be complex and uncertain, many organizational change programs fail to provide the benefits they hoped for, this can be due to many factors but insufficient attention to culture and the complexity of change can leave the recipients unwilling to accept new practices. If this happens the initiative will become unsustainable.

Many professional managers have experienced the frustration of introducing new practises, attending meetings, and gaining agreement only to find that with subsequent investigations many of the agreed action points have not been adopted and implemented. This phenomenon has been described in many ways including "agree and avoid" and "the art of non-compliance." Resistance to change can be deeply rooted in culture, with new practises and methods of working paying little attention to the requirements of culture in order to accept, promote, and sustain change within an organization.

Driven by the bottom line

A large number of management papers, articles, and theories have evolved regarding the importance and effective identification of organizational culture. For the purpose of this book we will focus on the cultural theoretical framework developed by Cameron and Quinn (1999).

The selection of this model serves both as the focus of this chapter and in the provision of a framework from which other models can be explored. The research also provides a compelling insight into the benefits to the commercial world of the importance of cultural management. Cameron and Quinn's book *Diagnosing and Changing Organizational Cultures – Based on the Competing Values Framework* (1999) is based on many years of extensive research into corporate performance. This research identified a number of illuminating observations including:

> Of the largest one hundred companies at the beginning of the 1900s, only sixteen are still in existence. Of the firms in the Fortune Magazine's first list of five hundred biggest companies, only twenty-nine firms would still be included. During the last decade, 46% of the Fortune's 500 dropped off the list.   (Cameron and Quinn, 1999, p. 6)

Their research illustrated the increased levels of volatility within large organizations. Although it would appear many companies are beginning to decline the moment they reach their optimum financial performance in the past this has taken many years. In the growing globalized economy the rise and fall of companies is becoming a far more rapid and volatile affair.

Cultural classification

Cameron and Quinn developed a model to help understand cultural mapping. This model is based on four cultural classifications around two opposing dimensions; the first dimension differentiates effectiveness criteria that emphasize flexibility, discretion, and dynamism from criteria that emphasize stability, order, and control. The second dimension differentiates effectiveness criteria that emphasize an internal orientation, integration, and unity from criteria that emphasize an external orientation, differentiation, and rivalry. The four cultural classifications were: "clan," "hierarchy," "market cultures," and "adhocracy." They emphasized that many organizations may have more than one or perhaps all of these cultural types present; the key is to be aware of their presence and deploy effective leadership and management strategies that make sure the organization's cultures are aligned to achieve the organization's aims and objectives.

These classifications represent attributes that individuals within those organizations believe are appropriate and promote behaviors aligned with the values associated with each category. Effective management often involves change and transformation in order to drive the business forward. Organizational transformation is a complex process that can be inhibited or inspired by individuals acting within an organization's society. Hence, the change process must take careful consideration of organizational culture in order to achieve successful management outcomes.

Culture and sub-cultures

The business practitioner must be able to understand the individual classifications within a cultural mapping model. This section illustrates how the British military culture maps across the model as an example. It is important to identify the multiple classifications and the importance of each culture's contribution to the functional performance of the sub-group or organizational state.

The four classifications match precisely the main organizational forms that have developed in organizational science. They also match key management theories about organizational success, approaches to organizational quality, leadership roles, and management skills. The first classification is the "hierarchy" culture.

Hierarchy culture

The hierarchy culture was based on the work of Max Weber (1947) who worked extensively with government organizations. He identified seven characteristics that have become synonymous with the classical attributes of a bureaucracy (rules, specialization, meritocracy, hierarchy, separate ownership, impersonality, and accountability).

The organizational characteristics focused on generating efficient, reliable, smooth flowing, and predictable output and therefore became the basic model for modern business management practice. This classification thrived in environments that are stable and tasks and functions are integrated and co-ordinated, where the uniformity in products and services is maintained and workers and jobs can be controlled. Clear lines of decision-making authority, standardized rules and procedures, controls and accountability mechanisms are valued as the keys to success.

The British military, in peacetime, focus on training, recruitment, and management would be closely aligned to this model. Many large stable organizations structure their leadership and management functions in keeping with this classification in order to produce maximum organizational efficiencies. It is important to note that this methodology creates the culture that is termed a hierarchy and is reflected in some degree in professional management practice.

The hierarchy culture is the domain of the professional manager with clearly defined rules and procedures. This commitment to excellence through standardization can be seen in organizations such as McDonald's with its relentless determination to produce standardized food and service delivery throughout its global fast food network. Similarly the Ford Motor Company was one of the earliest organizations to embrace mass production and highly centralized management methodologies. This has evolved into an organizational culture that we recognize as a hierarchy culture of today, many government departments also reflect this cultural profile.

The market culture

The market classification began to emerge during the 1960s and its definition is based on research of Williamson (1975) and Ouchi (1981) who suggested organizational effectiveness lay in controlling transaction costs. The market culture operates primarily through its economic mechanisms, mainly monetary exchange. The major focus of markets is to conduct transactions with other constituencies to create competitive advantage. Profitability, bottom-line results, strength in market niches, stretch targets, and a secure customer base are primary objectives of the organization. Not surprisingly, the core values that dominate market type organizations are competitiveness and productivity.

The increased popularity of strategic outsourcing is a typical manifestation of this kind of culture. The military outsourced many of its support functions, for example, accommodation, catering, transportation, facilities management, infrastructure development, and security services. The continued use of third-party suppliers to provide support or even core military functionality is set to continue and is driven through a market culture classification which often dominates procurement teams. The military has used the market approach in order to drive financial efficiency while promoting greater organizational agility through strategic contracting.

Companies like Philips Electronics undertook a significant culture change program following the loss of market share to competitors. The change program moved the company from a hierarchy culture to a market culture, placing the customer at the centre of cultural considerations. The hard driving CEO Jack Welch transformed many companies to reflect a market culture during his presidency of global General Electric (GE) during the 1980s, delivering significantly improved bottom-line results through customer engagement.

The clan culture

During the 1960s and 1970s the success of Japanese firms emerged and much of their success was ascribed to the "clan" culture. This culture focused on shared values, goals, cohesion, participation, and inclusiveness. The clan culture has been described as more akin to an extended family rather than an economic entity.

The military has the regimental tradition, which is very similar to the clan culture. The regimental family is a small unit of troops, (normally a group of battalions each comprising approximately 600 personnel) who share traditions, beliefs, and identity. They are loyal to each other and find external criticism very hard to accept. The concept of the regiment[1] is designed to allow rapid assimilation of new recruits, to make them feel part of a team that will support and encourage them, look after their needs, and to create an identity that is worth fighting for. These structures are found in the front-line units called "teeth arms" (infantry, artillery, and cavalry).

Cameron and Quinn's (1999, p. 46) research suggests that it is often found that:

> instead of the rules and procedures of hierarchies or the compet-itive profit centers of markets, typical characteristics of the clan type firms were teamwork, employee involvement programs, and corporate commitment to employees. These characteristics were evidenced in semi-autonomous work teams that received rewards on the basis of team (not individual) accomplishment and that hired and fired their own members, had quality circles that encouraged workers to voice suggestions regarding how to improve their own work performance and that of the company, and enjoyed an empowering environment.

Again these similarities can be found in infantry sub-units where teamwork, not individual performance, is recognized as a measure of success. It is often the case that a junior leader will be chastised if he/she succeeds and their team fails. Leaders are encouraged to involve the team in planning and individuals are given authority to carry out tasks without supervision. The level of empowerment is high within these sub-units and individuals are expected to act without asking permission and conduct their own analysis of what needs to be done.

Leaders are thought of as mentors perhaps even as parent figures and the organization is held together by loyalty and tradition. Commitment is high. The organization emphasizes the long-term benefits of individual development with high cohesion and morale being important. Success is defined in terms of internal climate and concern for people. The organization places a premium on teamwork, participation, and consensus. These qualities are important requirements for military units deployed on operations. The external threats that are constantly present require a culture that is inclusive, supportive, and loyal.

People Express Airlines and the John Lewis Partnership are examples of clan cultures that have developed strong individual commitment and have management behaviors that reflect a caring nurturing approach which are reflected in transactions and strong brand values.

The adhocracy culture

The final cultural classification of the model is termed the adhocracy culture. This reflects the hyper-turbulent, information rich global economy that requires a dynamic facilitative response. The adhocracy is an organization that promotes:

> innovation and pioneering initiatives that lead to success, these organizations are mainly in the business of developing new products and services. The major task of management is to foster entrepreneurship, creativity, and activity on the cutting edge. It is assumed that adaptation and innovation lead to the attraction of new resources and the improvement or maintenance of profitability. Emphasis is placed on creating a vision of the future.   (Cameron and Quinn, 1999, p. 38)

The British military deployed on operations and engaged in rapid adaptation within a hyper-turbulent context reflects many of the characteristics of the adhocracy culture. Leaders are focused on facilitating and empowering individuals to generate new ideas and innovate in order to provide competitive advantage within the operational context.

The adhocracy culture is characterized by a dynamic, entrepreneurial, and creative work place. People stick their necks out and take risks. Effective leadership is visionary, innovative, and risk oriented. The glue that holds the organization together is a commitment to experimentation and innovation. The emphasis is on being at the leading edge of new knowledge, products, and/or services. Readiness for change and meeting new challenges are important. The organization's long-term emphasis is on rapid growth and acquiring new resources. Success means producing unique and original products and services.

This culture is often exhibited in aerospace, software development, think-tank and consulting practices where innovation is highly respected. The resurrection of Apple's fortunes under Steve Jobs has reflected his commitment to an adhocracy that is focused on fostering innovation and creativity.

Cameron and Quinn's classification of cultural mapping is only one example of a number of cultural classification methodologies but it does provide a useful framework for illustrating how the British military has several cultures represented within the single organization and all with sub-cultures that are aligned with the output requirements.

Cameron and Quinn's model categorizes a number of cultural types and identifies the leader's values and management approaches that are typical of those cultures. However, it is important to note that no single culture is better than the next: the key is to develop an organizational culture which is appropriate for the wider competitive environment.

Improving operational performance

Using the same model to chart the separate sub-cultures of the British military illustrates the dynamic nature of its organizational culture and highlights how cultural management can have a significant high-performance effect.

As described previously, the British Army contains a number of cultural characteristics which vary depending on the functional requirements of the specific role being performed. Training, recruiting, and resource management reflect the hierarchy definition while operational deployment reflects the adhocracy cultural definition.

The competing values framework model can be used to plot an organization's profile. Many large organizations sit in several quadrants of the model, with sub-units or divisions displaying different cultural characteristics. The military display a predominantly two-dimensional bias occupying the traditional hierarchy cultural dimension for administration purposes while transiting to the more flexible and adaptive adhocracy for operations.

The military spends the majority of its organizational life within the hierarchy state, as this is the most effective command and control structure for a large organization. This traditional M form structure reflects many of the bureaucratic management methodologies that have become established practise in organizations today.

The cultural traits described would be easily recognized by any visitor to a military establishment. However, deployment to operational duties often sees the temporary organization develop a sub-culture that is underpinned by a clan culture. It plans and implements within an adhocracy methodology. This approach applies an N form methodology and achieves organizational agility and task appropriateness through task organization. The forces (political economic, resources, etc) and the task (operation task or mission to be achieved) combined with the limitations that are applied to the organization or force are usually the determining factors as to the mix of the cultural forms the deployed forces assume. These factors not only shape and influence the culture of the deployment force but will also determine the leadership style of the force.

The transition from one state to another (e.g. hierarchy to adhocracy) is often managed through a culture change program that is developed within pre-deployment training. Commanders and subordinates are trained under operational conditions to induce the circumstances where the cohesion and co-operation that will be required for the operation can be developed. This can involve a series of scenarios that the unit has not faced before.

They force the group to recognize the challenges and reflect on their present processes and procedures. Adaptation and culture change takes place as the team shares experiences and knowledge of new ways of working. The greatest achievement will be the readiness and flexibility of the unit to adapt to local conditions within a rapidly changing environment. The shift from proven procedures and rules to an acceptance of chaos and uncertainty is a fundamental requirement. It should be noted that different cultural needs have a direct impact on the leadership styles and methods that are required. At this point the leader is part of the team, developing culture and empowering individuals to make their own decisions within a decision framework that promotes unity of effort. The individuals must identify so strongly with the team and its values that they are willing to subjugate their own needs to the good of the whole. For this to be achieved the leader must exhibit traits which personify this enduring quality, that of servant leadership. This line of development fits very well with the "action-centered leadership model," used to develop officers at Sandhurst, based on the Adair (2003) model of three dimensions (task, team, and individual) and has been significant in focusing the military's approach towards leadership within an organizational framework. This combined thinking has significantly influenced the development of selection and training of leaders within the wider understanding of the context such as team and the task.

The move towards outsourcing and contracting of support services can similarly be identified as an organizational change between the hierarchy and the market culture. The catalyst or pre-deployment training is often facilitated by an external training team that will set the training conditions required for the task and often leads to greater innovation and empowerment of junior leaders with the organization. This operational flexibility is often lacking when the military tries to engage with external resources such as management consultants that identify and contract support services. There have been many high profile accounts of equipment debacles, which illustrate a failure to work together effectively. Where contracted services have been utilized, friction has often been created in the relationship between the military and contracting organization when the military moves into operational deployment. The contractor is not prepared for the flexibility that is required for this kind of transition. The system can function due to the comparatively little and limited time that the main bulk of the military organization spends on operational deployment. However, these relationships have been problematic when sustained operations have been required such as the Gulf II operation. The key issue that the military faces is that the organization is geared for war fighting capabilities – a requirement that is seldom needed. The new age of military operations has seen a greater emphasis on conflict intervention and management and as such calls into play different skills and processes.

The military has developed a communication system that enables the organization to analyze, communicate, and implement decisions rapidly. This has been in keeping with the contextual requirements of the organization's terms of reference. This may well be changing in the future where communications and virtual structures are required to fulfill the new types of task that future operations may hold. This suggests that as the organization's context becomes more complex it has a direct effect on the management methods and styles of leadership employed.

Arguably there may well be leaders who are fit for purpose; that is they exhibit the types of leadership qualities that best fit an organization within a given stage of its development. However, leaders may be specialists in change and this would introduce another style to the four previously mentioned. Kanter (1985) has long promoted the crucial importance of leaders as change agents, stating that all leaders must develop an understanding and high degree of competence in creating and managing change so that their organizations can survive. This statement would imply that all leaders need to have change capabilities as a core competence. Wheatley (1999) notes how change is the essence of the new global environment, and new leaders need to manage, not control, chaos. This recognizes that through any form of implementation process change is an inevitable factor and forms an important consideration within any such program.

Although this section has given prominence to the interactions between leadership, context and management processes, and the dynamics associated with the changes from hierarchy to adhocracy/clan cultures the military also has to contend with another scenario. In order for the military to conduct operations it also has to define, procure, and support equipment and services to the Front Line Commands (FLCs). The military, as part of a much larger Ministry of Defence (MoD), has to be able to transit from an operational culture (together with its systems, processes and imperatives) to a business space[2] culture that needs to be responsive enough to support military operations. Clearly, in terms of the overriding culture the MoD can be described as a bureaucratic, risk-averse organization. However, in order to help overcome a slow and methodical approach to equipment procurement the MoD moved to a structure of Integrated Project Teams (IPTs) where innovation, teamwork, and autonomy are the defining characteristics. In effect, this approach is a move to the clan culture with the IPT as the base unit. While this approach may seem like second nature to an army officer, it does not fit so well with other service personnel and certainly does not fit the traditional civil service culture. More recently it has become apparent that the delivery of operational effectiveness relies on a number of IPTs working collaboratively in order to deliver a military capability and that this is producing its own set of challenges. Not least of these is that the reward system favors success at the base-unit level rather than at the level of delivering the desired final state.

Over and above the MoD's day-to-day business when the military are on operations they find that they need the MoD machine to work much more quickly. This leads to the term, Urgent Operational Requirements (UORs) and in this case the MoD is able to slip into the adhocracy mode in order to deliver equipment upgrades and solutions to problems and in some cases new equipment very quickly. Often however, this is achieved at a cost premium but, it is argued, that cost is acceptable when the lives of service personnel and mission success are at stake.

When the operational emergency is over, the military staff find themselves having to manage the frustration of operating within the slow, risk adverse MoD machine. The only consolation they have is that their posting is likely to be for a maximum of two to three years after which they will be able to return to their regiment where they are more comfortable with the tempo and modes of operation.

Catalyst for success

The demands placed on an individual to respond to an emerging context requires processes, systems, and methodologies that support the individual to respond appropriately. These are enabled by the organizational culture and do not reside in the abstract. The selection of leadership based on shared values determines and molds the organizational culture, which permeates management practises, policies and procedures. When combined they result in an enduring organizational culture that is crystallized in the traditions that are upheld and recognized by all members of the organization. The British military has, over many years, evolved a culture, and a strong regimental tradition provides a foundation from which flexible responses can be deployed. However, they can also prove to be a key barrier to change.

The British military has developed and sustained a strong culture through the development of shared values that are expressed through the military covenant (written understanding of mutual commitment) shared history, traditions, and shared stories. The culture is cemented and sustained through a self-selecting homogenized community. Key is the individual's responsibility and commitment to the wider groups' interests and the subordination of their own.

The military has developed a process of using organizational tradition and culture as an effective foundation upon which they transform the sub-unit to an appropriate culture for current operations. This sub-unit culture produces a high-performing highly-optimized team but this operational culture cannot be maintained indefinitely because of the high levels of individual and collective performance standards required. The same cultural transformational process is used to reintegrate the deployed sub-unit into a steady, maintained state – this process is known as decompression.

Like an athlete preparing for competition, the British military carefully manages culture to produce optimized performance. Many of the top research and development (R&D) companies utilize the management of culture to create environments that promote new discoveries and innovation. Pharmaceutical companies have adopted cross-functional multidiscipline teams during new product development. This recognizes that cross-discipline thinking often provides the catalyst for critical analysis beyond the confines of a single scientific field and therefore provides approaches and solutions that are unconventional.

Importance of shared values

The military provides an excellent example of how culture can provide an adaptive foundation for transformational organizational performance. This functional output is achieved through a combination of organizational and capability agility, which provides the maximum utility of assets and this requires shared practices and leadership methodology, a common understanding, and widely understood functional tools. Central to this organizational elasticity is the promotion and maintenance of strong, shared values. These values provide the anchor from which transformation and adaptation can take place. Shared values bind the individual into a collective responsibility for action and a sense of ownership for outcomes. Many non-military organizations also have a strong sense of shared values – these can be within a vocational environment such as the NHS or embedded within a transformational organization such as Apple.

The deliberate manipulation of team sub-culture that takes place during pre-deployment training is carefully adhered to and promotes the core values of the organization. The process transforms around the values and adapts tools and methodologies; this morphs the organizational culture of the deployed unit to provide an appropriate functional output. Decompression provides the catalyst for the reintegration of the adaptive (N form deployed organization) back into an efficient management structure (M form). The leaders provide a critical role in setting the tone for this transformation; they must provide the example, the anchor from which the evolving team can retain a sound and resonating foundation from which they can innovate within the operational context.

Leadership living the values

During the process of organizational transformation a large number of tensions will emerge and will require careful and sensitive management by the leader. Many of these issues may be unforeseen and beyond the preparation, training, and experience of the leader. It is important that the leader has an inner foundation (strong values) on which they can base their decisions and actions in times of ambiguity.

The current and future operational context will remain complex and increasingly volatile. Organizations will require leaders to make decisions that have influence beyond their organizational confines in increasingly ambiguous environments. The dynamic extrapolation of tactical decisions into the strategic context requires an organization to share a common vision, a shared understanding that is reflected in its actions. This shared understanding (crystallized in its values and promoted within its culture) provides a consistent approach that gives the organization a robust operational framework. Even if the tactical decision proves, with hindsight, to be wrong, the organization is likely to be able to recover the initiative as long as it remains true to its values.

Policies in practise

An organization can be defined through it functional outputs and these are guided by policies and practises, all of which provide insight to the organization's soul.

All organizations have policies and practises. Increasingly these are carefully documented and in many cases reflect government legislation. However, the interpretation and application of these practises will reflect the inner values of the organization. It is often through the interpretation of policies and practises that promotion, rewards, and recognition are based and through which the individual gains a real sense of engagement with the organization. It is through this exchange that the individual is bound together with the organization's wider interest or in some cases feel disenfranchised.

The military has a number of procedural protocols as well as the sustaining procedures. They have also evolved a number of operational procedures and practises. These allow individuals and sub-groups to integrate seamlessly into other elements of the organization with minimum disruption. Although these augmented practises reflect the functional requirements of the task they are also supported by overarching organizational practises. These must be coherent with the values of the organization otherwise a disconnect between the message and sentiment and what the individual experiences will be different to the central values and propositions of the organization. Over time this tension will cause friction, doubt, and mistrust as the individual perceives a difference between the practise and preaching of the organization.

Through functional management and the product of staff work the leader must ensure that the policies and practises of the organization resonate with and reflect the core values of the organization and provide a useful bridge to maintaining a robust organizational culture.

Box 4.1 The John Lewis Partnership

John Lewis is one of the finest UK retail stores and has a prominent position in most of the UK's city high streets. John Lewis boasts a general purpose, retail store outlet offering a range of goods from clothing, furniture, electronics, toiletries to jewelry, as well as Waitrose, its high-quality food store, The motto, "never knowingly undersold," interpreted as the cheapest price for the highest quality of merchandise or food product, is lived daily in the partnership. The organizational structure of John Lewis reflects its financial structure; that of employee ownership. Some 50,000 plus employees own the impressive range of UK retail and food outlets. The culture is evidently service oriented, with politeness and helpfulness being two undisputable qualities staff display. In particular, the senior management decision-making structure reflects employee ownership and the philosophy of care and concern. Employee representatives sit together with top management shaping and setting strategy as well as diligently attending to all aspects of its service culture in order to ensure that the highest standards are maintained. Repeated customer surveys are testament to the fact that John Lewis clients note both the retail and food stores as second to none in terms of product quality, service, and aftercare.

The John Lewis highly acclaimed service culture was put to the test shortly after the tragic events of September 11, 2001. The fear in London was of a similar attack. Central London retail sales fell, with the John Lewis flagship store at the top of Oxford Street being badly hit. This was not a short-term, one-off, panic reaction. Over the months, sales did not improve. Central London was scared. Then the unthinkable; should the flagship store, the store where the John Lewis tradition began, be closed down? Despite the financial hemorrhaging, senior management decided that the future of the John Lewis, Oxford Street store should be put to the vote. A referendum with the following options was held:

A. All partners/employees (some 60,000 at the time) forgo their bonuses/pay rises (and in so doing pay for the Oxford Street store staff and overheads).
B. Close the Oxford Street store.

The culture of service and care was put to the test. The referendum result of all John Lewis employees was a 95 per cent plus in favor of forgoing bonuses and pay rises that year.

> We will not let our Oxford Street colleagues go to the wall.

John Lewis was not the best pay master in the sector. The vote was not one of discretionary spend. John Lewis staff and management needed their business/pay rises to face the challenges of daily living.

The Oxford Street store survived and prospers to this day. It remains the flagship of the John Lewis Partnership. The John Lewis culture of service and care is pivotal to the success of the organization and acts as a beacon for other organizations to emulate.

Development of high-performance teams

> *None of us is as smart as all of us.* (Blanchard, Zigarmi, and Zigarmi, 1985)

It is critical for the British Army's operational performance that it can effectively select and develop high-performing teams. These teams are prepared to perform specific tasks within an operational theater. Teams may be varied in composition and levels of specialization but the foundation and development process is highly structured to give an optimized performance when required. The military has also invested a great deal of time in decompressing these teams to bring high-performance teams down to a maintained training state similar to the way high-performance sports teams are treated. It is difficult to maintain individuals at high states of performance for sustained periods.

Optimizing performance through training

The British Army uses a highly-structured system of pre-deployment training to develop the team performance required for demanding operations. The process begins by focusing training at the individual level, providing everyone with high-level basic skills that provide a competency foundation on which specializations can be built. The next phase is the development of critical specialized skills required for sub-teams to remain balanced and to build flexibility at the lowest level. These may be specialist medical skills, driver training, signals, tracking, or linguistic skills. Developing individuals within the team to provide highly specialist capability enhances the whole team's utility within the wider operational context. This structured process of individual, team, and task has been summarized in Adair's (2003) work regarding an action-centered leadership model. Adair's reputation developed as a result of his theories regarding team development and his theories are widely used throughout military training establishments.

Performance under pressure

Individual teams (between four or eight soldiers and an NCO) are stress tested under a training environment to validate core skills and to mold the team into a single operating identity. Combining the team at this level is key; it is the leader's skill and judgment that identifies individuals who can work together. Matching personalities and capabilities to get the best from each other requires judgment and experience.

These small teams are then fused together to produce larger operational deployable units; other specialist teams augment the main body (logistic units, fire support units, civilian specialists, etc) in order to produce a force with organic capabilities to match the role they are deployed to. The structure of the force may vary from deployment to deployment as the operational requirements change; the changing configuration of capabilities is known as battle grouping and was first used by the German Army in World War II. In this agile organizational structure the role of leader and follower are interchangeable and reflect the contextual dynamics of the emerging situation. Organizations that need agile team response, such as oil exploration, new business functions, and rapid operational support teams would all benefit from this preparation.

My own experience was having responsibility for supporting large-scale consulting teams. These teams could be deployed at short notice anywhere in the world. They were cross-functional teams that had worked and trained together and they were supported by standard operating procedures that allowed different capabilities to be bolted together to provide the appropriate mix of capability for the consultancy assignment. This simple modular team approach provided world-class capability for very little investment cost. Duplication was kept to a minimum by ensuring teams operated to standard practices and this enabled individuals to move from team to team and immediately function effectively within a familiar framework.

Flexibility through shared practises

The development of specialized and interchangeable sub-units provides a high degree of organizational flexibility but it does require a homogenized culture and shared processes and methodologies that, in the military, are known as Standard Operational Procedures (SOPs). The development of a high-performance team is more than the adoption of a unified process and the British Army has defined a set of organizational values that attract and retain a group of individuals that share those values. These values provide a foundation that, through training and development, aid in the building of trust. Homogenized teams, drawn from the same culture and values build team performance and trust much more quickly than those teams that are not. This simple observation has wider implications for the selection and development of teams that are expected to perform within a highly competitive environment.

Building on the previous debate on trust, it is worth noting the importance of strong bonds of trust between team members. It is trust that allows individuals to take risks and subjugate their own personal objectives to those of the team. Building and sustaining trust is a critical requirement of the leader and consistent behaviors of the leader aid in establishing and maintaining trust among the team.

Values and trust are combined through an effective system of communication. The British Army has established a robust method of communication. First, the meaning of language is taught and specific words are given very precise meanings. This is often defined as mission language, words that if the precise meaning is not understood by all members of the organization then individual interpretation could have devastating consequences.

Box 4.2   The importance of precise language

An example of language being misunderstood within the military occurred during the Falklands War in 1982. The battle of Goose Green took place on the May 28 and 29. The 2nd Battalion of the Parachute Regiment was committed to a deliberate attack to capture Goose Green. The orders given by Brigadier Thompson were to conduct a raid on Goose Green. This was to be a simple probing attack with the main aim of gaining information. The raid was not intended to engage the enemy in any type of sustained action. The Commanding Officer of 2 PARA

Lieutenant Colonel Herbert "H" Jones VC interpreted those orders as a deliberate attack. The root of the problem lay in the lack (at the time) of shared terminology between the Navy and the Army. Brigadier Thompson was a Royal Marine Officer and as such served with the Royal Navy. A raid was recognized terminology within the service, but as the Army did not use the term, the misunderstanding left a space in which an individual's interpretation led to an operation that was never intended.

Learning culture

Through understanding the operational context the leader can assess the organizational culture and determine what needs to be done in order to be effective. The manipulation of culture can promote individual behaviors that help to achieve organizational goals. The nature of organizational culture is directly influenced through the selection of the leader. Leaders make decisions (especially when information is incomplete such as is often the case in volatile and complex environments) that are reflective of their inner-most values, what they believe to be the right thing to do. Therefore, the values of the leader directly affect organizational culture. Cameron and Quinn's research (1999) illustrates the importance of the right culture for the context, and that the selection of the leader against appropriate criteria which reflect values is critical in developing and maintaining that culture.

The military require a strong emphasis on empowerment and therefore trust is an essential attribute in order for the organization to function effectively within its dynamic context. Leaders that behave and make decisions in a consistent manner that promotes the development and sustainment of trust need to be selected.

In summary, the selection of leaders with strong shared values is critical as these combine to promote a strong shared culture that provides the foundation for operational transformation through the utilization of empowerment and limited risk taking implementation methodologies. The combination of these essential components provides the basis of competitive advantage in this complex hyper-turbulent environment. These practices have much wider utility beyond the military. However, they do require a radical re-evaluation of how organizations perceive and value their own organizational culture.

Notes

1. The original basis of the regimental structure was linked to the restoration of the Stuarts to the throne when the modern British Army was formed by Royal Warrant on January 26, 1661. The army expanded and contracted over many years to meet the needs of the nation. This was achieved through fostering small units with unique characteristics, often sponsored by a single individual (the Colonel of the Regiment). It was through this individualism that the regimental system was born.
2. While the term "business space" has been used in the past to define the activities of the MoD that support the military fighting capability, more recently this term has been replaced by the phrase "deep operations." The term has not been used in this book as it also has connotations of covert military activity and may cause confusion to the non-military reader.

CHAPTER 5

The tools of the trade

Throughout the history of conflict there have been examples of individuals who have seized the initiative and delivered victory from the jaws of defeat. These individual inspirational moments are a far cry from the deliberate identification, refinement, and adoption of a military doctrine that embraces empowered decision making in order to repeat this historical phenomenon for success.

This chapter will examine the historical background and context that inspired this formalized procedure that is now enshrined within Western military forces and commonly known as maneuverist warfare. The examination of the philosophy, procedures, and tools will illustrate the functional articulation of "how" the military implements this empowered approach.

This book began with the examination of transference of techniques and methodologies from the military to other fields of activity. Previous chapters have illustrated the foundation requirements of leadership, shared values, and strong cultures that promote trust and which are fundamental requirements that are needed before many of these approaches can be adopted successfully.

"No plan survives contact with the enemy": the roots of Mission Command

The doctrinal development of Mission Command as a unified structured approach can be identified during the early to mid-nineteenth century. Napoleon was at the height of his powers and leading a well-trained French Republic Army (Grande Armée) across much of Europe. On October 14, 1806 Napoleon's army engaged two Prussian armies at the battles of Jena and Auerstedt. Despite superior numbers the Prussians suffered a crushing defeat. The more flexible and agile[1] French forces were able to muster localized force superiority and deliver decisive engagements that won the battle. Napoleon marched on to bring much of Europe under his direct control. His staggering military success was due to a number of factors but his army's organizational and command agility enabled his forces to adapt to emerging situations and take advantage of fleeting opportunities.

The defeat of the Prussian armies at Jena and Auerstedt, gave rise to an in-depth review of the Prussian Army by General Scharnhorst (1755–1813), Gneisenau (1760–1831), and Carl von Clausewitz (1780–1831) all of whom served at the battle. Their first-hand experiences and observations convinced them that the secret of success lay in a more flexible response to situations. The review recognized the over-reliance on detailed planning that quickly became outdated and irrelevant once battle had commenced. The highly centralized and detailed staff procedures slowed the decision-making cycle to an uncompetitive level compared to the French system.

As a consequence of this review a revision to the 1788 Prussian Field Service Regulations was made in 1837. This stated, "If an execution of an order was rendered impossible, an officer should seek to act in line with the intention behind it" (see Oetting, 1993: 86–8).

This illustrates the move away from prescriptive orders based on a linear planning model to an acceptance of variability. Orders that could be interpreted based on the individual's reading of the situation were a radical departure from the then standard military practise. This authorized discretionary practise delinks the pursuit of the desired outcome from the prescriptive process of implementation. The conceptual jump defined the attainment of objectives through a descriptive effect, thus the use of intent combined the obedience to orders with the wider attainment of organizational objectives.

Such early insight was considerably developed by Field Marshal Helmuth Carl Bernhard Graf von Moltke (1800–1891) who is most popularly known for stating that "no plan survives contact with the enemy." His principal role was as the Chief of the General staff and as such he exercised a great deal of influence over the future development of doctrine and officer training.

It is in this post where Moltke had the greatest enduring influence. He believed in the selection and development of leaders who accepted responsibility and empowered subordinates and from this, over a period of time, an organizational culture that bred trust and commitment evolved.

This approach was captured in the 1869 new Field Service Regulations that stated that senior commanders should "Not order more than is absolutely necessary, but should ensure that the goal was clear. In case of doubt, subordinate commanders should seize the initiative" (see Bungay, 2005: 22–9).

The growing understanding of unpredictability (Clausewitz termed this friction in his lengthy study of the nature of war), complexity, and confusion also presented opportunity. Moltke recognized that planning was essential in mustering capability and direct action within a framework, however, the framework needed discretionary flexibility for opportunity to be turned into competitive advantage. To give greater clarity and direction Moltke observed that: "A higher intent had to unify action; and realization that every unit had to have a task or mission of its own to perform which made sense within that context" (Leistenschneider, 2002: 46–55).

This statement forms the beginning of deliberate terminology that became known as "mission language." Not only is the use and understanding of language very precise but also the structure of orders needs to combine the commander's intention with a specific mission set within the wider context. This sets the framework from which the individual commander can use discretionary judgment in order to adapt his mission to achieve the intent within a dynamic and emerging context that could not have been foreseen within the planning environment.

Empowering frontline staff to act independently within a framework reduces the requirement for centralized decision making. This concept would be further enhanced in the 1950s with the introduction of the Boyd cycle[2] or OODA loop significantly speeding up the organization's response time relative to the competition. This process has been greatly enhanced with the integration of technology through network-enabled platforms but the increase in information availability has also caused tension between command nodes and frontline commanders, with a natural desire for commanders to drill down into frontline commander's tactical operations.

The Prussian Army arrived at an intellectual crossroads guarded by two opposing schools of thought known as "Normaltaktiker" which believed in the detailed training of tactics and standard procedures for junior leaders and the other known as "Auftragstaktiker" which proposed that each situation was different and no standard formula could be adopted.

The dilemma the Prussian Army faced was that the only way to take advantage of chaos was to embrace the environment by developing a system of decentralized command that could take advantage of a rapidly developing situation. However, how can effective control be maintained without the entire organization descending into a chaotic state? As the Prussian Army became the German Army in 1871 a new concept of order emerged, "Discipline did not mean following orders but acting in accordance with intentions. The phrase 'thinking obedience' begins to emerge" (Bungay, 2005: 4).

The "Auftragstaktiker" school became accepted and was reflected in 1888 with the publishing of the new Field Service Regulations which stated that an officer should consider "What would my superior order me to do if he were in my position and knew what I know?"

This statement widened the parameters of discretion and confirmed the German approach. This lengthy explanation of the historical roots of Mission Command serves to illustrate the incremental, grounded approach that the German Army undertook. This liberalized approach gained wider acceptance after the German military's impressive performance during the 1918 spring offensive and the tactical performance of the Wehrmacht army during World War II but was only seriously studied and gained acceptance by other Western armies when they were faced with the dilemma of the Cold War.

Mission Command has been refined further in recent years and is articulated in army publications:

> Mission Command is a philosophy of command, with centralized intent and decentralized execution, that is

particularly suitable for complex, dynamic and adversarial situations. A maneuverist approach demands a philosophy of command that promotes freedom of action and initiative. Like a maneuverist approach, Mission Command focuses on outcomes, as it stresses the importance of understanding what effect is to be achieved, rather than specifying the ways by which it should be achieved. It has the following key elements:

- A commander gives his orders in a manner that ensures that his subordinates understand his intentions (**intent**), their own **missions**, and the **context** of those missions.
- Subordinates are told what **effect** they are to achieve and the reason **why** it is required.
- Subordinates are allocated sufficient **resources** to carry out their missions.
- A commander uses the minimum level of control possible so as not to unnecessarily constrain his subordinates' **freedom of action**.
- Subordinates then **decide how best** to achieve their missions. They have a fundamental responsibility to act in line with their commander's intent.
- In order to apply mission command subordinates must adhere to six key principles, these are:

1. Unity of Effort
2. A Specified Main Effort (analysis)
3. Freedom of Action (empowerment)
4. Trust (leadership and culture)
5. Mutual Understanding (standardized approaches)
6. Timely and Effective Decision-Making (OODA loops)

(British Army, 2010, pp. 6-11–6-12, section 0.621)

Mission Command and a maneuverist approach

Mission Command can be attributed to the reflective thinking of the Prussian staff after the unexpected defeats at Jena and Auerstedt. However, the evolution of maneuver warfare was aided by analytical study of successful military campaigns that often saw a more mobile, agile, and well-trained force defeat a numerically stronger adversary. During the 1980s the Western armies faced just such an adversary, the study of the dilemma culminated in the synthesis of the operational philosophy of a maneuverist approach[3] and its key constituents are:

- An attitude of mind – it is based on being able to understand and manipulate human nature in order to identify vulnerabilities and points of influence.
- Practical knowledge – requires a broad fund of practical professional knowledge based on individual education and collective training.
- A philosophy of command – is underpinned by a command philosophy of centralized intent and decentralized execution that promotes freedom of action and initiative (Mission Command). (adapted from British Army, 2010, chapter 5)

The maneuverist approach is applied through the following five key attributes:

- Understanding the situation
- Influencing perceptions
- Seizing and holding the initiative
- Breaking cohesion and will
- Protecting cohesion and will

Each attribute is further broken down but such a detailed examination of the maneuverist approach and its application to modern warfare falls beyond the scope of this book. However, it is important to note the critical relationship between the maneuverist approach (military approach to conducting current operations) and its dependency on Mission Command's leadership philosophy.

The moving sands of time

The development of maneuver warfare culminated towards the end of the Cold War, its powerful effect was graphically illustrated during the 1990 Gulf War – operation Desert Storm with the overwhelming destruction of Saddam Hussein's forces in a ground campaign that lasted only 100 hours.

Although the maneuverist approach had demonstrated its worth during the first Gulf War, as so often before, the changing world would soon challenge extant thinking. In 1991 the former Yugoslavia erupted into a succession of bitter internal conflicts marked by internal tensions between ethnically divided communities. Soon the West was involved (via a UN mandate) in complex operations with the aim of enforcing peace and rebuilding states. The demands of peacekeeping and capacity building within a wider national framework challenged the extant operational philosophy. General Sir Rupert Smith (UN commander during the Bosnia conflict) termed the phrase "war among the people" to describe the emerging conflict context, which centered activity within communities.

The complexity of the military mission in the Yugoslavian conflict forced the West to re-examine its military philosophy. While the maneuverist approach provided a proven methodology for exploiting technologically-advanced and highly-trained forces against numerically superior forces in a high-intensity kinetic environment it did not account for the increasingly complex and volatile asymmetric and delineated battlefield that was emerging.

The military recognized that they needed to consider the context beyond the immediate conflict situation. The analysis of any mission or task needed to consider the implications of action in a much broader context. Planners needed to consider the foundations of the problem in order to build an appropriate response that could transcend the immediate conflict and look deeper into how to solve the friction that underlay the manifestation of conflict. This more expansive thinking became known as the comprehensive approach.[4]

The emerging thinking behind the comprehensive approach quickly recognized that a great deal of the capability and influence would be provided by non-military organizations but it also recognized that the catalyst for change and the organizational planning infrastructure would most likely be provided by some form of military component.[5] As comprehensive thinking evolved the friction between centralized control (command paradigm) and an individual organization's terms of reference, cultures, and individual leadership and management processes[6] provided a significant hurdle to integration. While this work continues the military has now incorporated the comprehensive approach into its analysis and planning process to ensure that the potential problems are considered if not resolved.

The framework and impetus for the comprehensive approach was set within a European context and has subsequently been challenged and examined in greater detail in more recent operational environments (Iraq and Afghanistan) but the central premise that expansive thinking must be applied in order to resolve and provide a sustainable solution to future conflicts remains intact. The evolution of the maneuverist approach, enabled through Mission Command and evaluated through a comprehensive framework required a transparent and robust analysis and decision-making process to manage the complexity and provide an audit trail for action.

Within the military the notion of a comprehensive approach when developing a capability or going on operations has been captured in the concept of the defense lines of development (DLODs) which have grown in recent years and now consist of eight elements. The actual elements cover: training, equipment, personnel, infrastructure, doctrine/concepts, organization, information and logistics and are known by the acronym TEPIDOIL. The key point is that all elements have a role to play in being able to deliver a military capability and depending on the nature of the issue at hand the weighting of each element will vary. As widely reported in the press some years ago the UK's MoD purchased Apache Helicopters only to discover that the training element had not been fully thought through and as a result the helicopter was ready but not the pilots.

The notion of thinking through the first and second order effects is not peculiar to the military. For example, any business that is launching a new product will need to consider the implications on manufacturing capacity, technology readiness levels, the sales force, the distribution structures, the impact of seasonality on cash flow requirements, coherence with branding position, and the list goes on and on. Failure to consider the wide range of dependencies and interdependencies will more often than not result in a sub-optimal result at best and total failure at worst. In some cases history shows that a company can get it so very wrong in this regard that it results in the total failure of the company.

On the military front the comprehensive approach represents a significant challenge at a national level where the government of the day has a fair degree of control over resources and decision making. However, the levels of complexity increase in order of magnitude when military action involves multiple nations. For example, when the operation is under NATO control there are standards and protocols that actors have signed up to and so the actual military operation can be conducted in a co-ordinated way. As we have seen in Iraq and Afghanistan the military element can be but the tip of the iceberg and the real challenges begin when the reconstruction and stabilization elements are being addressed. Since NATO does not have a remit to hold a civilian standing force it is required to work with government organizations, charities, non-governmental organizations (NGOs) and a raft of other third parties (including privately- and publicly-owned companies) and this brings with it a number of agendas. For example, many NGOs will only engage in the operation when they have a semi-permissive environment but at the same time if they are working in a situation where they are seen together with military they themselves become a target. Unfortunately, the nature of conflict today is such that the enemy does not simply surrender and allow the reconstruction to go ahead in a non-threatening environment (as might have been the case at the end of World War II). The threats today that are being confronted in places such as Afghanistan are enduring and any particular part of the country can find itself a battleground today, relatively peaceful tomorrow, and back to a battleground the day after, such is the nature of insurgency and terrorism. The terror comes from the uncertainty and the fact that it prevents people getting on with their lives and building a future.

Some might argue that the comprehensive approach could equally be described as the commonsense approach and one only needs to turn to any text on strategic management or strategic marketing to see how they highlight the importance of understanding your stakeholders and recognizing the differences in organizational and national cultures. It is only through this approach that one can craft a strategy that will enable organizations to work together with a common goal and purpose and have in place approaches and processes to manage the friction points, that is, points where reasonable alignment cannot be achieved. The real challenge at present with the adoption of the comprehensive approach is that there is yet to be sufficient alignment between key organizations as to a definition of the very approach itself. This is despite the fact that at summits, for example, in Riga and Lisbon, the heads of states all agreed that this makes sense and progress must be made if nations are to be able to work together effectively.

It's all relative!

Anyone who has been involved in business and has worked for a number of organizations will have seen that when it comes to strategy formulation and decision making there is no "one size fits all" answer. Experience shows that some organizations will make decisions on the hoof, while others will make an industry out of gathering data and conducting analysis to the point of "analysis paralysis." Often the approach may come down to the ownership structure of the company in question or the leadership style of the person(s) at the helm. In order to set the scene against which to compare the approach adopted by the military it is appropriate to ground this section on the basis of a medium to large size company that has a degree of functional structures and processes upon which decisions are made.

The academic literature presents the reader with many tools and techniques that have utility in any organization in helping management make sound decisions that can be traced through a logical process. For example, the development of a marketing plan will involve the consideration of many factors such as the organization's current position in the market, the nature of the competitive environment (to the point of analyzing competitors strategies), consumer research in terms of identifying critical success factors, the strengths and weaknesses of one's own organization and that of the competitors, the nature of the macro environment and the dynamics of the industry. This list represents the starting point only for any organization when embarking on a strategy formulation process.

The key point to note is that with the move to the "planning school" that took place in the 1970s there was no shortage of tools and techniques for the manager to apply. Many of these were developed by management consulting firms of the day and used as a basis for selling their services – the likes of the Boston Box and the McKinsey screen come to mind in this regard. A key point to note with all of these tools is that they do not provide the manager with answers, rather, they are a means to cross check propositions and help management ask the right questions. When applied with a degree of rigor, management are better placed to understand where the organization is currently positioned (this has a bearing on what it is able to achieve), the art of the possible, and a sense of how the journey can be completed. However, as with the concept of the comprehensive approach, the real challenge for management is in being able to recognize the dependencies and interdependencies within the value chain in terms of converting base resources into a viable product and in delivering it to an informed customer. In the case of a publicly quoted company the purpose is to increase shareholder value, or in the case of a public sector organization to be able to deliver a service efficiently and effectively.

Clearly in most organizations management strives to deliver benefits, however, it is also the case that many confounding factors come into play ranging from egos, internal and external politics, and more often than not a lack of management expectation . As often quoted in marketing texts, the biggest mistake one can make is to "over promise and under deliver" and yet it happens time and time again.

The final point to note is that one should not underestimate the importance of leadership (at all levels within the organization) in ensuring that a robust decision-making process is in place and that appropriate analytical tools and techniques are applied in a fair and open-minded spirit that results in a comprehensive approach to decision-making in an environment of trust, integrity, and common purpose.

As Mission Command enabled decentralized decision-making and empowerment to improve the opportunity for competitive advantage, the concept of the decision/action cycle or OODA loop had a significant impact on how we think about decisions. Although Colonel John Boyd analyzed the phenomena through his experiences as an F-86 pilot during the Korean War the net contribution recognized the importance of making quicker decisions comparative to your opponent.

If a decision methodology could be adopted at the lowest appropriate level of the organization the cumulative effect would be to outperform your opponent. Imagine two boxers, one large, powerful, and slow, the other quick, nimble, and maneuverable. Although the larger opponent possesses considerable destructive power he will find it difficult to bring that power to bear as the quicker fighter out maneuvers his opponent through "reading" his opponent's actions then uses his agility to move out of the way and land his own punches as and when he chooses. If this process is repeated with increased tempo eventually the bigger fighter will be overwhelmed by his opponent's style. In this example the quicker boxer can read and make decisions faster than his opponent. This scenario combines quicker cognitive processes with a more agile physical response to make a formidable adversary. It is this combination that the military attempts to emulate in its thinking, organizational agility, and decentralized decision-making. Figure 5.1 illustrates the decision/action cycle. However, it should be noted that although the illustration portrays a successive process it does not have to follow this – analysis and decisions can jump from one element of the process to another.

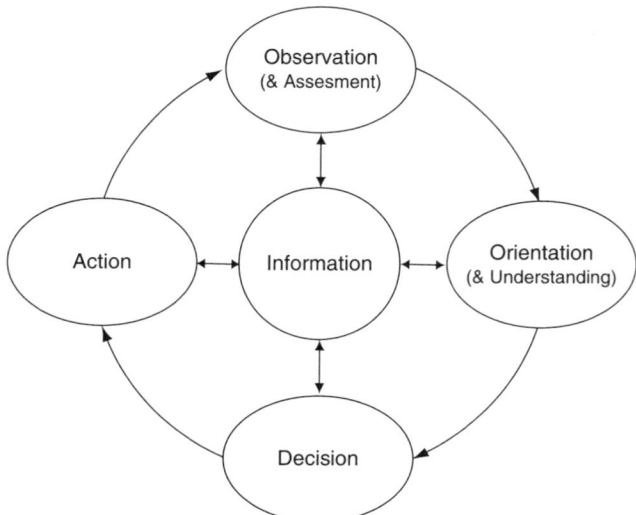

Figure 5.1   The decision/action cycle

Source: Adapted from the OODA loop diagram by John Boyd; see British Army (2010).

Box 5.1   The consultant from Search and Rescue

One of London's outstanding strategy consultants was asked, "Why do the clients keep coming back to you? Why are you successful?"

It only took a moment's reflection, "Well it was when I was an RAF helicopter search and rescue pilot."

In his normal quiet, unassuming style, the consultant outlined his philosophy, "I was told I was a pretty good pilot not because I got better marks in training but because I read the situation well."

He continued, "I remember one dangerous mission where we had to rescue two sailors stranded on rocks at the bottom of massive stone cliff in a storm with sea waves lashing the cliff edge ferociously. They should have returned to harbor but instead their yacht was smashed against the rocks and the two miraculously scrambled onto the cliff bottom. In that storm, I had to judge how to hold the helicopter steady while it hovered over the two and judge the fear and motivation of my crew to do the job when the chances were we could all have been smashed against the cliff face. There was me judging wind speed (it was bad), desperately trying to control the helicopter, give orders about when to winch down and get the two and show calm leadership to all around. I remember shouting – 'our mission – we save lives – are we all on board?' There was no hesitation from the crew – 'Yeh!' We saved the lives of the two. We went home all safe. We used that experience for training in the future."

The consultant paused for a moment. "And that is what I do now. The mission is clear but each situation is different. The team knows the mission but we all throw our bit in with each client we have. We speak bluntly and are better for it. The clients know that even if we have a template, we treat each one as unique."

Again he paused, "Do you know what the real test of all this is? – I have never sold anything to anyone and yet my diary is always full."

Seeing inside your head

The military utilize a structured, cascade approach to problem solving recognizing that the higher the level of command the greater is the level of complexity. In order to aid the commander three levels of estimates[7] are utilized: first the operational estimate, second the tactical estimate, and third the combat estimate. All three are linked and have been designed to take the product (output) from one level to "feed" the next level of analysis. Through this cascade approach individuals can understand the context and the assumptions that have predicated the estimate formulation.

Operational estimate

The operational estimate employs a six-step methodology and its aim is to situate the military analysis within the wider operational context. In order to achieve this wider view it employs a comprehensive outlook and aims to identify the "underlying themes" as well as the operational issues. The six steps in broad outline are as follows:

1. understand the operating environment (framing the problem)
2. understand the problem
   a. mission analysis
   b. evaluate objects and factors, and
   c. the commander's confirmation
3. formulate potential courses of action (CoAs)
4. develop and validate CoAs
5. evaluate courses of actions
6. the commander's decision.

Each step of the estimate is broken down to provide the commander and his staff with a set of tools that can be applied to understand the complexities of the problem. The methodology of the operational estimate is mirrored within the combat estimate but the issues that are considered are far broader within the operational estimate.

Tactical estimate

The tactical estimate follows the same format as the operational estimate and is designed to allow the commander to focus on the tactical problem. By understanding the operational estimate the commander can appreciate how the higher commander has considered and arrived at his own decision (wider considerations may impose constraints or tasks that must be achieved that otherwise may not appear obvious if only the tactical issues had been considered). The six steps of the tactical estimate are:

1. review the situation
2. identify and analyze the problem (mission analysis and initial object analysis)
3. formulate potential CoAs
4. develop and validate CoAs
5. evaluate CoAs
6. the commander's decision.

Combat estimate

The combat estimate is the most widely utilized estimate process, it focuses the commander on problems at the combat (localized) level. It is a flexible process that can be expanded to incorporate higher levels of complexity or collapsed to provide a quick checklist for a commander under pressure. The seven questions (or steps) are:

1. What is the enemy (adversary) doing and why and/or what situation do I face and why, and what effect do they have on me?
2. What have I been told to do and why?
3. What effects do I need to have on the enemy (adversary) or situation, and what direction must I give to develop the plan?
4. Where can I best accomplish each action or effect?
5. What resources do I need to accomplish each action or effect?
6. When and where do the actions take place in relation to each other?
7. What control measures do I need to impose?

The three levels of estimate knit together to provide a strong analytical and deductive process that links the wider thinking of the comprehensive approach down to tactical (everyday) relevance. The philosophy of mission command encourages individuals to use discretion in order to achieve the desired outcomes.

As described throughout this book the military has evolved a number of methodologies and processes and have invested in selecting leaders in order to build a supportive culture of success. No individual component can stand alone or provide a winning formula without being integrated with the other techniques.

With this in mind a number of other concepts need to be considered in order to review the whole and understand the connected nature of the military approach.

Effects-based planning

During the estimate process a number of "products" are produced which culminate in a plan. The military utilizes a system of defining a goal through the description of an "effect." This provides a description of the end to be achieved rather than the resources needed to achieve the goal. Effects-based planning defines future objectives within an ambiguous context and thus provides the commander with greater latitude as to how to achieve the effect. As the context evolves the assessment of how best to achieve the effect will constantly be reviewed. A number of unforeseen events may well present the opportunity for the desired effect to be achieved without the implementation of the original plan. Effects definitions are at the heart of the estimate process as it is the effect that needs to be analyzed within the emerging context.

What's in a word? Language and meaning

Good quality communication is essential in military operations as sharing understanding and giving direction in this highly pressured environment leaves little margin of error. The military have evolved a system (orders and back briefs) that provides a formulaic structure for communications. The structure and process of orders is well understood by all members of the military and significantly reduces ambiguity or misunderstanding that otherwise may arise within this complex environment.

To supplement orders the military use a system of "back briefs." This is a process where a subordinate is tasked with briefing the task or emerging situation back to their superior. This process confirms understanding and allows the subordinate to interrogate, clarify, and interpret the problem in order to gain greater understanding.

To aid the communication process the use of defined and precise language is utilized to convey meaning. This is described as "mission language" and provides a definition of language to give clarity to tasks.

Box 5.2   Bridging the leadership chasm

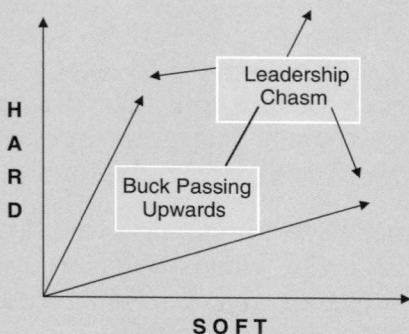

Figure 5.2   The leadership chasm

A top management program was being held at the Executive Development Centre, Cranfield School of Management, UK. The client was a well-known international portfolio company, with businesses varying from niche, specialist services to volume, commodity goods. The participants were the senior managers from each of the businesses. The session was on leadership and the discussion on the challenges each manager would face in their job. The concern was on how to bridge the likely lacuna of leadership when a manager is asked to pursue two contrasting demands simultaneously, namely trying to make hard and soft synergies work, and is unable to do so!

The hard strategic synergies are costs or organization structure. The soft strategic synergies are quality of service provision, collaboration in the supply chain, and partnerships. The reason for gathering this eminent group of top managers at Cranfield was to explore and arrive at a shared view on the competitive advantage of the conglomerate. No one notion of competitive advantage could be identified as each of the businesses in the portfolio was, not only distinctly different to the other, but also at different stages of maturity in the economic life cycle. No focal point could be found; so how to be more focused?

The Group Finance Director spoke, "What we say is right! We do not have a focal point that brings us together."

The comment surprised everyone. For the first time the Group was admitting no clear way forward as opposed to its normal style of driving hard to meet targets. "How do you cut costs, sack people, and then motivate the rest to work as a cohesive team, guaranteeing their future when you have just made their mates redundant?"

The same Finance Director was now in full flow, "What we have learnt today is that when a job is so impossible, managers are paralyzed, don't know what to do, do nothing and then buck pass upwards. If that is true then we need a World Class Corporate centre to lead the way. Who here thinks we have such a center in the group?"

No movement and not a word. Silence meant no trust in the Center.

"Neither do I. So let me tell you what Finance is going to do. We are going to drive and consult. We are going to police and be a friend. I am going to do both the hard and soft so that everyone else can see what needs to be done. Your job is going to be to tell me whether I am doing that well or not."

The other senior managers looked at each other in amazement. Is this Finance talking?

"The language is consultative," finished the Finance Director, "that's going to be our competitive advantage. We will realize synergies that our competitors think impossible!"

He meant it. Finance became consultative while being as directional as ever. Soon those half opportunities that line managers had thought were not worth considering became the success stories of the new entrepreneurial culture. In the various boardrooms of the group, the lexicon of the corporation was focused on four words; synergy, hard, soft, and consultative.

Organizational agility

As discussed previously the military utilize "task organization" as a method for maximizing the efficient use of resources. Task organization allows the organization to be designed for the specific task, providing specialist skills and concentrated capability at points when they are needed most. This process supports the maneuverist approach and depends on a unified working methodology.

To provide the "plug and play" task organizational capability it is imperative that specialist units can be integrated quickly into a formation for a specific task then be quickly reassigned to other formations where their specialist capabilities are needed. The military utilize standard formation operational procedures to ensure units can quickly be assimilated into the operational methodology of the formation.

The sum of the parts

The military have developed an approach to conflict that requires a highly flexible organization and leaders who can cope with ambiguity and identify and seize opportunities as they emerge. The processes and tools that have been highlighted in this chapter provide an integrated system for coping with and exploiting complex and volatile environments. The previous chapters have highlighted the foundation requirements upon which these tools, methodologies, and flexible processes can be deployed.

Key themes in summary

The military have defined their process and approach to optimize performance within a highly complex and volatile environment. The key themes identified could be adapted to meet the growing demands in other non-military organizations and the following should be considered:

A structured process for understanding and analyzing complex problems This process should be utilized throughout the organization providing transparency and an effective foundation for justifying decisions. The process should be flexible in order to deal with different levels of complexity.

Development and considerations of alternative options The process should produce a variety of options to solve a given problem. These should be considered, evaluated, and role-played to find the best option and evaluate alternatives that may need to be considered if the original plan does not meet with the anticipated success.

Employ an implementation methodology that is robust and flexible This is particularly necessary in the face of changing situations. In the military, as in business, situations change rapidly and careful consideration should be given to giving greater discretionary powers to implementation teams who are often best situated to understand the emerging nature of the problem.

Use defined language and confirm understanding Communications are critical to successful outcomes. Building and sustaining robust methods of communication will vary from organization to organization. However, it is important that an appropriate structure, content, and process is considered and integrated into business practice. Staff should be encouraged to "back brief" to confirm understanding and provide situational awareness for superiors.

Evolve flexible structures that maximize the efficient use of resources and provide an agile response to changing situations A number of business structures are based on standard organizational design, however, an opportunity exists to look more imaginatively at aligning structures against the operational reality of the competitive environment. This places a greater burden on leadership and management processes.

Identification of leaders who can be developed into effective managers The leaders should be capable of leading and empowering wider groups of people to identify and exploit opportunities within the work place.

Notes

1. Combining the organizational design of the Corps structure that contained units of dedicated cavalry, artillery, infantry, logistics, and so forth, these formations were capable of independent action and enjoyed a degree of decentralized command. The French staff system was also more flexible and dynamic than other armies of the day. Later, many of these principles were absorbed into modern military thinking known as maneuver warfare, which will be explained in more detail later in this chapter.

2. This phenomenon was first formally observed by a retired US Air Force Colonel John Boyd, who studied the American air superiority in the Korean War. Although the Chinese were equipped with the superior Russian MiG-15, the Americans with their inferior F-86 enjoyed a 10:1 kill ratio. This was due to some technical differences that allowed the American pilots to achieve greater observation and more maneuverability. Boyd identified (Pech and Durden, 2003) that the F-86 pilots followed a process where they observed where they were relative to their enemy, orientated themselves on the basis of their observations, made a decision to act, and then put that decision into effect. The pilot would then observe and reorient relative to his enemy, decide on his next action, and then repeat the process. The F-86 pilot would continue the cycle until the opponent became disorientated and lost control. This same phenomenon has been identified in land warfare. Lind (1985) claims that Boyd's study of ground combat identified a similar pattern: where one side would present the other with a sudden, unexpected change, or a series of such changes to which the other side could not adjust, resulting in defeat, usually at small cost to the victor. Boyd found that the loser had often been physically stronger than the winner, but the loser had suffered panic and paralysis similar to that experienced by the North Korean and Chinese pilots.

3. This is an indirect approach that emphasizes understanding and targeting the conceptual and moral components of an adversary's fighting power

as well as attacking the physical component. Influencing perceptions and breaking or protecting cohesion and will are essential. The approach involves using, or threatening to use, force in combinations of violent and non-violent means. It concentrates on seizing the initiative and applying strength against weakness and vulnerability while protecting the same on our own side (British Army, 2010).

4. Although military forces – often land forces – can play the decisive part in a campaign, crisis management (the process of preventing, containing or resolving crises) needs active interagency engagement, using all three instruments of power – military, economic, and diplomatic – in order to succeed. A comprehensive approach requires proactive engagement, shared understanding, thinking based on the outcome rather than the input, and collaborative working (British Army, 2010).

5. The key military role is usually to create the conditions for the other two to work, or to work better, either by fighting or by helping to stabilize the situation. It is governance, economics and better lives, facilitated and explained by diplomacy, that provide lasting campaign success (British Army, 2010).

6. One of the challenges for a fully effective interagency approach is that organizations have different planning processes, attitudes to sharing information, and varying lead times for action (British Army, 2010).

7. An estimate is a logical process of reasoning by which a commander, faced with an ill-structured problem, arrives at a decision for a course of action to be taken in order to achieve his mission (DCDC, 2008).

CHAPTER 6

You've got to find what you love: engagement beyond transaction

This chapter draws together the key themes and discusses the interconnections and mutuality of the constituent topics. The chapter draws to a close with a brief discussion regarding the wider implication of values-based leadership within the global context and illustrates the importance of understanding the significance between operational activity and global strategic themes. It is critically important that leaders understand the wider context and the significance of activity within this framework in order to provide appropriate and sustainable leadership.

How many people will get out of bed on a Monday morning dreading the week ahead, feeling no engagement with the corporate body except a begrudging existence of financial servitude. Another week to be endured in order to financially survive and provide the glimpsing opportunities for self-expression and engagement that so many individuals crave and are so often only achieved in part time activities? Steve Jobs (newly appointed CEO for Apple) said at the graduation of Harvard students in 2005:

> You've got to find what you love, and that is as true for work as it is for your lovers. Your work is going to fill a large part of your life, and the only way to be truly satisfied is to do what you believe is great work, and the only way to do great work is to love what you do. If you haven't found it yet, keep looking, and don't settle. As with all matters of the heart, you'll know when you find it, and like any great relationship it just gets better and better as the years roll on. So keep looking.

Steve Jobs' comments were poignant because he had only recently been declared in remission from a long fight with pancreatic cancer, a fight that he would eventually lose in 2011. His comments reflect the wider context and the lack of engagement individuals feel in many of today's organizations. The desire for individuals to feel valued and included is a deep-rooted human need. The root of the problem can be traced to many modern business management practises.

Many societal and business structures are led and managed through a transactional management methodology. This approach does not create engagement or commitment on the part of the ordinary workers and has demonstrated its potential for self-serving interests and a consolidation of power in an increasingly small proportion of the population. This crystallization of control is difficult to justify when the performance of those organizations suffer under this leadership approach. The problem is compounded when the benefits that the few enjoy are derived from the resources of the wider society.

Of course this situation does not cover the totality of society and there are many organizations and vocations that provide tremendous scope for an individual to make a contribution that is highly valued. For example, most of the work undertaken by charities, while often not well paid, can be extremely rewarding and fulfilling. Work in research establishments can be extremely challenging but again equally satisfying when a breakthrough is achieved which will make a real difference to the lives of thousands of people. Having said this it is still the case that for the majority of staff in paid employment the scope for job enrichment and job satisfaction is more limited than need be and that middle and senior management leadership can have a significant role to play in establishing a valued community environment.

In support of this line of reasoning the military has evolved a values-based approach to leadership and those values are expressed across the wider organization. This approach promotes the wider interest of the group and the importance of teamwork and shared reward. This nurturing style has proved to be both transformational and sustainable even in the toughest environments.

It is important to note that leadership does not preside in an abstract stand-alone context; it requires shared understanding, a common language, authority, legitimacy, and consistent behaviors that build trust in order to be effective and sustainable. These attributes need to be considered carefully within the organizational context and the systems/processes within the organization need to be supportive of the approach and built into the leadership philosophy.

The organizational leadership paradigm must look beyond the boundaries of the immediate situation so that they can resonate and respond to wider problems and opportunities. A comprehensive conceptual approach towards analysis and action needs to be adopted by senior leaders in order to provide strategic direction for organizational agility in a way that is fully comprehended by those throughout the organization.

As the global economy and national borders become even more pressurized much could be learnt from the military's approach.

The importance of values, past, present, and future!

The evolution of society with its ever increasingly sophisticated interdependency of specialized tasks and skills necessitates the requirement for capturing the value of the exchange process.[1] This need has been crystallized in the concept of "value" and provides the basis for economic transactions. The interdependency of social advancement has been inextricably linked to the development of economic theory and practise. Knowledge evolution, acquisition, and exchange provide the basis for new theory development and once applied in practise, this synthesis has provided a powerful combination for social progression.

This interwoven and interdependent relationship has been underpinned by the beliefs and values of society, which are reflected within the exchange process. As an example, even as late as the Middle Ages, both Christian and Muslim societies prohibited the loaning of money for the purpose of gaining wealth or "interest." However, without access to this vital funding (particularly for trade), society found its economic interests limited.

For a further example, we need look no further than Shakespeare's *The Merchant of Venice*, which depicts Shylock in an unfavorable light. However, the Jewish communities (whose religious beliefs did not preclude the loan of money) played a vital role in every major city of the day, providing the capitalist structures and essential funds required for trade expansion. This example illustrates how societies evolved new methods of satisfying their economic expansion by circumnavigating religious and legal practices of the day, and so the ebb and flow of social, economic, political, and legal practise have evolved together and because of each other.

Although the evolution of capital has been incremental and emerging, it has produced two very different models today. The first is the shareholder model, most common in the established economies such as the US, UK, Australasia, and much of Europe. This model is increasingly driven by short-term return. The global economy has facilitated new opportunities for the movement of debt and the realization of unsustainable short-term returns. It is this methodology of inflated value that underpinned the financial crisis of 2008 and beyond. The second is social capital that focuses on long-term investment and can be found in Germany, Japan, and the Far East. It can be difficult to delineate the two models. At times a useful point of departure can be identified as the end of World War II. Many of the victorious countries were driven to supercharge economic shareholder transactions, while defeated countries needed to rethink their economic model and bring together their communities in order to provide the foundation for reconstruction. This "hard reset" produced a different model for capital economics with a focus on long-term investment and shared returns (because the finances came from society as opposed to the international capital markets). Today we stand at a crossroads; with a global financial model on the verge of collapse and a few economic silos that stand alone. These beacons are all based on social capital economics that were evolved from a strong vision and values framework.

Box 6.1   The moral position of capital

The event was a recent international conference in London. The theme was "The Global Recovery: The Steps to Take." The speakers comprised of an array of academics, top businessmen, and politicians from the House of Commons and Lords. Each offered their views concerning the causes of the global financial crisis (GFC) and the steps to take for recovery. Frankly, the audience had become bored. They had heard all this before.

The audience of more than 600 had waited for the speakers who were scheduled for the last two slots of the afternoon. One was a well-known, hard-line, financier and member of the House of Lords, the other a well-known academic whose views on recovery from the recession contrasted with most of the day's speakers.

"The quicker we take the pain of the cuts we need to make, the quicker we will move out of recession," said the Lord.

"Health service cuts are absolutely necessary. The elderly have to be provided for by their families and their communities. With an ageing population looming, the state cannot afford to provide for so many. We are on the verge of bankruptcy. This could tip us over."

The Lord in question continued his theme of cutting costs, as the prime lever for reducing debt so that the financial markets gained confidence to invest and trade. This speaker was formidable in his use of language and construction of ideas. Agree or disagree with him, he was difficult to challenge. Not surprisingly, his talk was followed by no questions.

"And then what," began the academic.

"So the City and Wall Street gain their confidence and then what? What will they do with the capital available?"

The academic paused, looking around to the audience and throwing the occasional glaring glance at his fellow speaker.

"They will invest in exactly the same financial instruments, the derivatives, futures, real estate, that led us into this financial crisis. We will then have an even bigger crisis because all the reserves, we the citizens could have, will have been used up paying this present mountain of debt."

The Lord made to jump in and offer comment. The Chairman of the forum stopped him and beckoned the academic to continue.

"We have privatized gain!"

"We have socialized debt!"

"We have privatized vulnerability!"

Again the academic paused for effect.

"In other words, all the money that we in this audience made, no matter how hard you guys work, the bankers and funds keep! All their debts you lot pay for! And when you lot become ill and old, you pay for it despite the fact that the bankers and funds have so much money!"

The Lord was having no more of this, "What you say destroys the entrepreneurial culture of this nation. You and those like you have made public services so top heavy, no private sector could ever pay for this!"

"No, it is you and your thinking that are destroying the nation! You allow short-term transactions, speculation in effect, on high rates of return to dominate the life of this nation. This makes the rich become richer and the rest of us poorer. All that the life of the citizen is worth is transaction cost economies, in other words my life and those here at this conference, are worth nothing more than deals that just line your pockets. We need to invest in information technology on a long-term basis. All the capital that this nation has could be used to invest in education, care for the elderly, alternative sources of energy, even streamline transport. We need a 25–30 year, long-term infrastructure plan with investments at reasonable rates of interest. Nobody can become too rich but no one will be poor."

"This is communism", glared the Lord.

"No," retorted the academic, "this is the struggle between shareholder capitalism and socialized capital. Both have a market focus philosophy underlying them. The former requires the corporation as the vehicle for wealth creation. The latter requires partnership between government and capital in order to invest in long-term infrastructure projects. With socialized capital, innovation will come from the far more agile family businesses rather than the aggressive but sterile corporation seeking to satisfy only its ends through rent seeking behavior!"

"This is not practical! This is not a way forward. What you say will incur such turbulence, this nation will be even worse off", stated the Lord.

"No, not the nation, but just you and your lot in the City! And why are you so surprised, Germany and China are the two prime examples of socialized capital. The Anglo Americans are the epitome of shareholder capitalism. Which of these two models do you think is sustainable? Which do you think will survive into the future?"

The academic turned to the audience, "Which do you think is sustainable?"

No reply.

The academic continued, "If Europe were to become one country, they would naturally adapt the German economic and political model. The citizens would be far more engaged, jobs would be in abundance."

The academic was not allowed to finish. The Lord was already spitting venom. Europe to become one nation? That was just too much.

The academic retorted in an equally aggressive manner. The two just went for each other. The Chairman had lost control. The audience was forgotten.

It became clear to all that the values underlying the positions the two had adopted were irreconcilable. The more they challenged each other, the more they ground themselves into their own bunkers. The audience shifted around uncomfortably. They too were divided, approximately 50/50 in support of the two speakers.

The discomfort of the audience however, was more due to the sharp retorts between the two speakers and the sense that there was little to negotiate. You were either on one side or the other.

The deadlock was broken by a rather timid question from a middle-aged woman in the audience.

"I am Chairman of a Health Authority. Why are we being forced to choose between the two of you?" she asked.

"Why is there no middle way?"

The academic jumped in quickly, "Which middle way do you want? Please tell me where is that middle position? This is what happens when a whole society is allowed to deteriorate to the point where the only option is a stark choice between two competing and contrasting values."

He looked at the audience, "What does anybody do when two leaders, with two contrasting points of view, claim that there is only one way forward? How does one negotiate between two fundamental value positions?

The Lord was about to question just what the hell the academic was talking about.

The academic simply glared at him. If the two of them had guns, they would probably have shot each other.

The Chairman, unable to cope with the animosity of the room called the meeting to a close, thanking both speakers for their contributions.

The two departed without even looking at each other. The customary handshake after the exchange was noticeably absent.

A key catalyst for social and economic evolution has been the exchange of knowledge, that is, ideas put into practice and shared across a group to expand the collective capacity. The method of knowledge exchange has evolved from word of mouth to books, through to the invention of the telephone and relatively new capabilities such as the Internet. The relatively free access to the Internet has widened the access and publishing capabilities for the individual, enabling greater diversity of ideas and innovation. This liberalization of knowledge exchange has in turn evolved new ways of organizing resources and marshalling capabilities.

The vast majority of today's organizations are designed in order to try to maximize efficiency. These multidivisional, centrally controlled, hierarchical management structures reflect the most current business management thinking and practice and are classified as "M form" organizations.

These structures are being challenged by "N form" designs, which are fluid, task-oriented transient organizational structures that morph according to task and shared community interest. This real-time collaborative design is challenging traditional models and providing N form organizations with asymmetrical capabilities in the sense that a relatively small group can organize in an organic manner that makes it very difficult for a traditional organization to be able to respond effectively. Clear examples of this include Al Qaeda and the Arab Spring uprisings. This was visible in the UK student riots where social networks were used as a method of organizing individuals. They collected and shared knowledge in real-time providing better situational awareness than the police force. This allowed the students to outmaneuver the police and achieve disruptive protests and maximum attention.

The Internet and social networks were again used as critical information and organizational frameworks for protests during the Arab Spring. The liberalization of knowledge exchange has provided the opportunity for social asymmetric capabilities beyond the established and accepted old social structures of business or state organizational design. N form thinking is beginning to permeate across the boundaries of established M form thinking, and typified by strategic outsourcing, contracting, and the proliferation of consultants for specialist knowledge. It is beginning

to break down the traditional line boundaries of the organization, producing a more blurred interaction and organizational
relationship, accessing key skills and knowledge and capabilities that traditionally would not have been available within traditional M form organizational thinking.

This is part of the evolutionary process of social change that
has taken place throughout history, with technological developments acting as a catalyst for change. Yet, although technology
is becoming more widespread, the high-tech, knowledge-based
economies are evolving at such a pace that the net effect is the
creation of a new age of third world economies – a world that
is based on technology rich and technology poor nations. The
access and exploitation of information technology and the
advancements that this capability facilitates, produces greater
innovation and rapid implementation by improved knowledge
exchange. It is perhaps not surprising that national governments
are desperately trying to impose control over this valuable
source of social interaction. As technology access needs capital
investment, it requires capital markets to invest in order to produce the landscape from which knowledge can be accessed and
utilized. Perhaps it is not governments, but capital markets, that
will impose the ultimate control over the evolution of societies.

Societies are complex and dynamic, resources need to be allocated and individuals need to work together. They, therefore,
require organizing. This need will ensure the retention of M form
structures but ones that need to think and have access to N form
capabilities in order to remain competitive. A new form of management is called for, one that is adaptive and empowered in
order to capture the collective capability of the social network.
The military has embraced a leadership and management philosophy termed "Mission Command" that takes advantage of
complexity and volatility by empowering the wider community
to make decisions from a common framework of understanding, bound together and sustained by strong cultural and leadership values. Mission Command provides a methodology for
bridging the gap between the highly structured M form and the
decentralized N form, providing both control and discretion.

Too many organizations, particularly in the public sector, focus
on "doing things right." Values-based leadership provides a

powerful narrative as it reflects the inner beliefs of society in general and the organization in particular. Its outputs and management functions naturally embrace the framework of "doing the right thing," however, this philosophy can become insular and selective in closed societies. In a world of interconnected communications and trade, do global values exist and can they evolve in harmony with each other?

Growing talent and commitment

In the ever increasingly hyper-competitive global environment, the need to optimize the skills/capabilities of the organization and the need to access network capability in order to achieve competitive advantage is an increasingly critical requirement for success. Engaging all aspects of the organization is more than empowerment; it is a process of building trust and commitment from which leaders can empower subordinates and subordinates will accept responsibility, ownership, and accountability for that empowerment.

Engagement is multidimensional. Not only does it require nurturing between individuals but it must also consider the wider network of stakeholders and in the process develop a methodical and sustainable process of engagement that has the ability to grow beyond the individual and connect with the wider network to produce high levels of commitment and innovation.

Leveraging the capabilities of the extended social networks of organizations has a force multiplying effect. Not only are you gaining more from your organization, you are extending this contribution to your own engaged community beyond the boundaries of the organization. Many organizations are now actively promoting the use of network development. Traditionally, this has been through networking meetings where people meet face-to-face. More recently it has become evident this is being facilitated through business social networking sites such as LinkedIn. Active networking is being driven much deeper and wider across the organization. The various groups and forums offer opportunities for individuals to find answers to problems, access new talent, and share knowledge.

Understanding how second- and third-order networks interact is an increasingly important management issue. The military has been forced to look at virtual networking capability because of recent military operations in places like Iraq and Afghanistan.

Insurgent groups such as Al-Qaeda are employing this capability in order to achieve asymmetric operational performance. It is interesting to note that social networks self-organize, that is to say that the network self-selects and self-profiles over a period of time. Communities that share a particular interest attract others who share that interest. Through analysis, a profile can be created around interaction of interest which provides a much more qualitative insight as to the networks' capability and influence. Second, the structure/profile of a network is different from the noise or information and interaction the network generates. For example, the context of the activity (internal and/or external) can itself be the basis for the stimulation that sets the agenda for the structure/profile of the network. The power of these networks can be experienced in a number of ways and can shape an agenda intellectually or result in some physical activity or even provide a more subtle role in influencing stakeholders – irrespective of the outcome it is the case that networks need to be seen as something that require a degree of management. The contribution towards and the benefits received by individuals are not evenly shared and require skilful manipulation in order to maximize benefits for a particular interest or purpose. Third, networks rapidly evolve and change (shape, dominance, and capability). Leadership is transient; the group is engaged but influenced through key individuals and/or events. This eclectic environment requires leaders who can influence, shape, and evolve a narrative that permeates complex networks and transcends the ripples and complexity of contextual emerging events.

Businesses and state functions are rapidly developing network capabilities within and beyond the traditional boundaries of the organization. Understanding and influencing this evolution will increase the opportunity for leveraging competitive advantage from these extended network capabilities. The military's experiences in Afghanistan and Iraq have highlighted the importance of identifying and understanding the full potential of networks. The Taliban improvized explosive device (IED) campaign has proven to be so effective that the Western coalition have decided to target upstream of the problem. They actively analyze networks in order to identify the most effective targeting of military assets. Identifying key individuals within the wider network has a force multiplying disruptive effect.

This dynamic environment provides new challenges for leadership thinking, no longer can leadership be expressed through a command and control paradigm alone such as the management structure found in traditional M form organizations. It must be adaptive and inclusive to carry the masses with its aims and objectives; the message must resonate over a number of complex issues and circumstances in order to circumnavigate the complexities of the emerging context and harness the full potential of the N form.

Values-based, people-centric thinking: building communities of common interest

It is an old adage that "an organization's greatest asset is its people." However, management action seldom reflects this fact. Increasingly, the volatility and complexity of the environment will demand more of individuals to act, contribute, and be engaged in the active management of the organizations they are connected to. Creating social engagement must highlight the importance of the individual contribution. Placing the individual's interest within the community of supportive shared views, values, and desired outcomes builds commitment to a common goal. The role of the leader is to embody these individual and collective needs, while management action should reflect these values.

Giving individuals a strong sense of belonging provides the foundation of a sense of community cohesion. The individual feels they are part of something bigger, something that will endure beyond their own time. The military spend considerable time and effort in building a strong sense of belonging, based around the regimental tradition. This sense of belonging builds a strong culture that is resilient and committed to success. Leaders need to reflect the common values of the group and act for the good of the whole community. This connectivity is critical in maintaining legitimacy of leadership authority. Leaders who reflect the shared values of the group attract great commitment and engagement from the community.

However, one also has to recognize that within a military context this position is facilitated by the fact that the "day job" puts lives at risk and that every member of the team knows this and fully realizes that if they do not do their part a colleague may fall. Such thinking extends along the line from the "teeth" (the fighting elements) to the "tail" (the supply and support chain) and as such is comprehensive within the organizational construct.

Communities with strong values identify quickly with each other. They have a shared understanding of right and wrong and can build a strong sense of trust between individuals and leaders who reflect those qualities. From this basis of trust, individuals are prepared to take risks on behalf of the wider community. They understand the group's limitations and expectations. The group's values provide the parameters that guide behaviors and set expectations. A word of warning, when a leader does not act in a way that reflects the shared interests of the community or exhibits behaviors that are not reflective of the team, an inner friction is created that must be resolved, the leader must be replaced or the community fragments.

Mission Command thinking linking M and N form organizational capability

The requirements of the competitive environment mean that organizations need to optimize all organizational assets. However, empowering individuals involves risk. The military discovered that instantaneous mass media added complexity and operational volatility. Increasingly, the actions of an isolated individual could have strategic consequences and shape the future outcome of the campaign. This issue could not be ignored and the friction between centralized and decentralized decision-making provided a dilemma. The M form organizational desire for centralized management control became increasingly redundant. Recent military operational experiences in the complex and volatile space of a delineated battlefield have required greater agility; more devolved decision-making and organizational risk to be managed through shared values and a common understanding. Increasingly, the value of a hybrid organizational design (M form central structures for organizational needs and N form interfaces for engagement and tactical agility) is beginning to emerge. The utilization of "Mission Command thinking" facilitates this decentralization of decision making that enables localized networks to evolve. A limited hybrid organization design has been utilized in recent operations, however, its conscious design and active management is not fully understood and is viewed through an abstract lens in the context of a specific operation. Mission Command thinking has provided the centralized M form with the opportunity to exploit its organizational systems of scientific management to maximize efficiency, while the empowered nature of Mission Command operational delivery philosophy exploits the flexibility of the N form. Perhaps only through retrospective analysis will organizational understanding emerge.

The recent experiences of protracted operations have highlighted the importance of understanding values and the different nature of social values. The difficulties understanding the complexities of social values constructs has fed friction with localized commanders struggling to find common ground and to build unified commitment in order to deliver operational success. In short, if the solution is not recognized and owned by the indigenous population the change will fail to be sustained, therefore the end state must resonate and reflect the indigenous population's values set.

A world that recognizes the importance of values must learn to accept other value frameworks or pursue a methodology of domination and conquest. The international community is based largely on Western Christian values which may well be challenged in the emerging global context of the financial crisis and with the rise and fall of economic empires. For example, the radical Islamic fundamentalist movements believe in promoting a 1,000 year Caliphate (system of Islamic Government) and the long-standing tradition of Buddhism and Taoism have a profound influence on the emerging perspective of China and Far Eastern countries.

Throughout history, there have been many examples of strong values-based leadership, where individuals, with enduring legacies have helped shape our understanding of a resonating narrative that engages the whole community. From the inspiring Christian work of Mother Teresa in the Indian ghettos, to the sinister leadership of Joseph Stalin and Adolf Hitler, they each drew on wider social beliefs to create engagement. They developed rhetoric that touched people's lives, persuaded them that individual sacrifice and extreme hardship was the transformational price of delivering the vision of the future. Values-based leadership is a powerful leadership philosophy and one that can drive societies forward, to greatness or the very edge of destruction.

Investing in leadership at all levels

As outlined in this chapter, the demanding requirements of leading in difficult and ambiguous environments demand much of the leader. Defining the requirements and selecting against those needs are fundamental to success. Technical skills can be trained, management functions can be learnt but values-based leadership demands that the leader possesses and believes in the values of the organization. As a significant proportion of decisions and behaviors are informed by and reflect our innermost beliefs, it is essential that the leaders must share the organization's values. If they do not, then regardless of their managerial expertise, their decisions and behaviors will not resonate with the wider community and leadership legitimacy will be eroded. Therefore, leaders should be selected with an emphasis on identifying appropriate values; management skills should then be trained and developed.

> On this rock I will build my church; and the gates of hell shall not prevail against it.   (Matthew 16:18)

The military has evolved an incremental grounded approach to retaining competitive advantage. It has studied its opponents and attempted to optimize all aspects of its organization in order to achieve relative comparative advantage; that is to say, be better than your opponent where it counts. It is important to establish a culture of understanding competitive relativity, that is, to make sure that everyone is engaged in thinking and acting more quickly and effectively than their opponent, this way, the organization will collectively outperform the competition. This can be reflected in organizational structures, decision-making and management processes but essentially, it is an attitude of mind.

Understanding the organization's culture is the key to understanding the organization's capabilities, what it stands for, what it is prepared to do, and how resilient it will be to the turbulence and challenges faced in order to be successful.

Cultures are reflections of values. Culture grows and it is embedded over time. It can be visibly identified in traditions, customs, and accepted methods of doing everyday tasks but it is also embedded in the unspoken, unobserved traditions and rituals of the individuals that occupy and sustain the culture itself. This unspoken, unwritten understanding of culture is the most powerful attribute of culture. It provides the individual understanding and commitment to the organization. It is important that the foundation and source of culture is built on transparent and shared values that act as a binding glue in challenging times.

Change management must understand the importance of how to recognize, decode, and work with organizational culture for successful outcomes to be achieved. Recent military operations have recognized the importance of cultural differences and have begun to shape the military response to achieving campaign success. Perhaps this will become a strategic consideration before military operations are conducted in the future. To change an organization or nation state, a long-term plan and commitment needs to be constructed. UN and NATO missions are increasing in size and length to reflect these underlying challenges and intervention must consider this significant commitment before operations commence.

Intervention requires a clear understanding of what is to be achieved and recognition that ultimately the indigenous population can only sustain the change that is brought about by that intervention. Therefore, the change must consider the culture and organizational values that exist today and to what level the new change will resonate with those established values. It is important to recognize the difference between management and process change and the fundamental values and beliefs from which these systems are supported and sustained. The concept of democracy, as understood by the Western powers, may not be universally supported or wanted by other nations with different values. To impose this system requires such significant change that successful outcomes are unlikely. One might consider the US's view of democracy in light of the challenges they have faced in trying to facilitate "state building," the answer lies in the fact that the view of a democracy can only be defined by those who are actually going to live there and for whom it will be their way of life.

However, culture can also be a powerful tool in leading change. If the change can be owned and embedded as part of the organization's own values, reflecting a desire for a shared common goal, then the change program has a high chance of success. Identifying and understanding common "touch points," rhythms, practises, and language build the framework for common understanding. Establishing and working within widely shared practices enables dialog and common understanding. These sub-structures also enable engagement and facilitation. The military utilize SOP to draw the different constituents of the formation together and create a common framework for operational cohesion. Organizational cultures will have similar systems (although not so well developed or categorized) and these are the points within the organization that are understood to be the methods of communication and shared understanding. Utilizing existing structures and facilitating the creation of new ones is a key requirement for the manipulation and transformation of cultures.

Creating purposeful organizations: tents instead of cities

The procedures and methodologies that an organization employs provide windows to its culture and values. The military utilize common analytical and decision-making processes, providing transparency and an auditable trail for how decisions are made and outcomes are arrived at. Individuals are taught to be accountable for decisions and understand responsibility. Organizations should utilize common tools and procedures that are readily accessible, understood, and utilized throughout the entire organization. These tools and procedures must be appropriate for the operational environment and be reflective of the considerations of the values of the leadership and organizational paradigm.

Useful and accessible tools and procedures provide the framework from which true creativity and original thought can be established. They provide the methodology for mundane (but essential) consideration and evaluation. They deconstruct the clutter that could otherwise add to the complexity of the problem and provide the synthesis for effective decision-making and the platform for inspired leadership.

The shifting sands of the global economy challenge the requirements of establishing and maintaining dedicated resources. Task organization establishes the conceptual framework from which organizational and network capability can be optimized for efficiency and flexibility, creating an agile organizational response to an emerging context. This approach requires common understanding, a shared language, and a focused response to problem solving.

Summary

The world is rapidly changing and the recent economic crisis has illustrated the fragility of our present economic model. Leadership has been eroded and replaced with self-serving management interest. This situation is of our own creation. We have encouraged a social model that has become increasingly insular. This is reflected in our capital and political structures that look inward instead of outward. Numerous scandals have rocked society's belief in the present leadership model. We are rapidly approaching a tipping point. Increased social dissatisfaction is beginning to manifest itself in fringe social issues. The growing discourse within our social structures, compounded by the world shift in economic and political power, is creating a dangerous imbalance to our old established model.

Much of this book has examined key leadership and management issues at the operational level; however, these are a crystallization of strategic themes that link to wider contextual considerations.

Leadership and management action must be situated in the operational context but must also be aware of the strategic thematic influences in order to provide appropriate and interpretive leadership.

Understanding the connections between the operational and strategic frameworks is important to enable the effective recognition of positive and negative action, for example, a positive effect at the operational level of removing a dictator and the negative strategic impact of destabilizing a region. If we briefly consider the events in Libya – the overthrow of Colonel Gaddafi, a ruthless dictator for over 40 years, ruled Libya with an iron first and exerted huge influence through his control of significant oil reserves. The social unrest within the Arab states spilt over into events in Libya that led to the overthrow of the dictator. However, while the direct action of Western military capability was very evident, less obvious but equally influential was the continuous lobbying of all the major world powers who were busy protecting their own national interests. So the dictator has gone but the aftermath has left a less-well structured society that has bigger issues than the direct control and protection of its most important asset – its oil. Libya can be viewed through a justifiable and positive operational act that helped liberate a population, however, understanding the strategic imperative of destabilization of the wider region in order to secure favorable access to oil reserves cannot be ignored if effective leadership is to emerge.

The control and manipulation of the global economy is an extension of the national (wider society) influence through foreign policy but also more significantly through the strategic application of economic interests. It is understandable that societies protect their own interests and utilize all means to pursue their own interests and expressed agendas. However, the danger becomes acute if these strategic decisions do not consider the values of the societies they claim to represent; this is the dilemma between the friction of social and capital interests.

The enduring nature of values permeates our individual and collective decision making; they influence our acceptance of operational action. The tension that exists in a global economy with different values sets has not yet crystallized within the operational context. However, there are signs that the strategic struggle for values domination has been at play for many hundreds of years. It is unlikely that global values will be recognized as independent desirable states, the struggle for domination and assimilation will continue. It is understandable and predictable that the Western globally dominated capital structure will protect its own interests.

The access to technology has liberalized knowledge exchange at the operational level, however, the polarization and rapid development of new technology has become a strategic imperative, the gap between the developed and developing world is growing larger not smaller. The utilization and control of the knowledge economy is a decisive and critical strategic issue that is well under way. Technology is but one element in the strategic thematic tapestry; energy, water, health, and food are some of the other issues that are actively managed in order to deliver the wider strategic objectives.

The leader must understand the broader context and the key themes that shape and direct the operational context. For leadership to be enduring and decisions sustainable the leader must be able to access the values foundations of groups and apply the strategic influences in order to provide a pathway for development. The nature and types of leaders are critical, this is beyond the simple dimension of people management or charisma, the recognition of operational and strategic leadership must be unified through shared values connectivity.

A re-evaluation of our social model is required. Simply, do we want leaders and political and economic structures that exist and reflect the wider requirements of our social needs or not? Leadership and success should be rewarded but not at the expense of the communities they serve and that they derive their support and revenue from. The strategic and operational actions of our national interests should resonate and make sense. This alignment with values will ensure that the wider social interest is served.

The military has provided a useful case study, a lens for consideration, a different model based on the same social values and needs as the rest of the West, but different emphasis is given to leadership, risk, reward, and culture. Could this provide some insight as to the future shape of the Western political and economic model?

Note

1. In some ways this is an extension of the Michael Porter value chain model which is basically an economic approach to establishing the value of each activity undertaken by the organization. The military model clearly addresses the economic value added issue but also views value from a social standpoint and the contributions individuals make to the team and that teams make to the organization. It should come as no surprise that the term "taking one for the team" has military origins.

REFERENCES

Adair, J.E. *The Inspirational Leader; How to Motivate, Encourage and Achieve Success* (London: Kogan Page, 2003).

Blanchard, K.H., Zigarmi, P., and Zigarmi, D. *Leadership and the One Minute Manager: Increasing Effectiveness through Situational Leadership* (New York: Morrow, 1985).

British Army *Values and Standards of the British Army* available at: http://www.army.mod.uk/documents/general/v_s_of_the_british_army.pdf (Army Doctrine Publication, 2008).

British Army *Operations* available at: http://www.mod.uk/NR/rdonlyres/41903E11-B6F4-4351-853B-2C1C2839FE1B/0/ADPOperationsDec10.pdf (Army Doctrine Publication, 2010).

British Military's Command Model, Vol. 2, Army Code No 71564 (Army Doctrine Publication, 1995, pp. 1–3).

Bungay, S. (2005) "The Road to Mission Command: The Genesis of a Command Philosophy." *British Army Review*, 137 (Summer 2005): 22–29.

Cameron, K.S., and Quinn, R.E. *Diagnosing and Changing Organizational Culture* (Reading, MA: Addison-Wesley Publishing Company, Inc, 1999).

Collins, J., and Porras, J. *Built to Last: Successful Habits of Visionary Companies* (New York: Harper, 1994).

Davies, J.B., Sandstrom, S., Shorrocks, A., and Wolff, E.N. *The World Distribution of Household Wealth* (Helsinki: World Institute for Development Economics Research, 2006).

DCDC *5.00 Campaign Planning* 2nd edn available at: http://www.mod.uk/NR/rdonlyres/56AAAE6B-0728-4D10-A6AB-DBBE30B957B8/0/JDP5002ndEdCh1web.pdf (Joint Doctrine Publication, 2008).

Fayol, H. *Administration Industrielle et Générale/General and Industrial Management* (London: Pitman, 1916).

Hargreaves, D. (2011) *What are We Paying For? Exploring Executive Pay and Performance* available at: http://highpaycommission.co.uk/wp-content/uploads/2011/09/HPC-DPperformance.pdf (London: The High Pay Commission, 2011, p. 4).

Jobs, S. *Harvard Commencement Speech* available at: http://news.stanford.edu/news/2005/june15/jobs-061505.html (Stanford University, 2005).

Kanter, R.M. *The Change Master* (New York: Simon & Schuster, 1985).

Kiszely, J., and Royal United Services Institute for Defence and Security Studies. *Coalition Command in Contemporary Operations* (London: Royal United Services Institute, 2008).

Krzyzewski, M. Coach of the United States men's national basketball team 2008 Summer Olympics, available at: http://dailycelebrations.com/070401.htm (2011).

Leistenschneider, S. *Auftragstaktik im preußisch-deutschen Heer 1871 bis 1914* (Hamburg: Mittler, 2002, pp. 46–55).

Lind, W.S. *Maneuver Warfare Handbook* (Boulder, CO: Westview Press, 1985).

MOD *Design for Military Operations – The British Military Doctrine 1996* Army Code No 71451 (1996).

Nietzsche, F.W. Aphorism 146 from *Beyond Good and Evil* (Leipzig, 1886).

Oetting, D. *Auftragstaktik – Geschichte und Gegenwart einer Führungskonzeption*, (Frankfurt-am-Main: Report Verlag, 1993).

Ouchi, W.G. *Theory Z: How American Business Can Meet the Japanese Challenge* (Reading, MA: Addison-Wesley, 1981).

Pech, R.J., and Durden, G. "Manoeuvre warfare: A new military paradigm for business decision making". *Management Decision*, 41, no. 2 (2003): 168–179.

President Abraham Lincoln "Letter to Col. William F. Elkins, November 21, 1864." *The Abraham Lincoln Encyclopedia* (New York: Macmillan, 1950).

Probst, P., and Raisch, S. "Organizational Crisis: The Logic of Failure." *Academy of Management Executive*, 19, no. 1 (2005): 94.

Shankleman, M. (2008) "UK income gap 'same as in 1991'" BBC News, available at: http://news.bbc.co.uk/1/hi/business/7786149.stm (December 16, 2008).

Smith, General Sir Rupert *The Utility of Force* (London: Allen Lane, 2005).

Taylor, F.W. (1903) *Shop Management* (New York: Harper, 1903).

Weber, M. *The Theory of Social and Economic Reform* [trans A.M. Henderson and T. Parson] (New York: Free Press, 1947).

Wheatley, M.J. *Leadership and the New Science – Discovering Order in a Chaotic World* (San Francisco: Berrett-Koehler Publishers, 1999).

Williamson, O. *Markets and Hierarchies, Analysis and Antitrust Implications: A Study in the Economics of Internal Organization* (New York: Free Press, 1975).